Uproar in the House

A Farcical comedy by

Anthony Marriott and
Alistair Foot

WWW.SAMUELFRENCH.CO.UK
WWW.SAMUELFRENCH.COM

Copyright © 1973 Anthony Marriott and Alistair Foot
All Rights Reserved

UPROAR IN THE HOUSE is fully protected under the copyright laws of the British Commonwealth, including Canada, the United States of America, and all other countries of the Copyright Union. All rights, including professional and amateur stage productions, recitation, lecturing, public reading, motion picture, radio broadcasting, television and the rights of translation into foreign languages are strictly reserved.

ISBN 978-0-573-11468-7

www.samuelfrench-london.co.uk
www.samuelfrench.com

FOR AMATEUR PRODUCTION ENQUIRIES

UNITED KINGDOM AND WORLD
EXCLUDING NORTH AMERICA
plays@SamuelFrench-London.co.uk
020 7255 4302/01

Each title is subject to availability from Samuel French,
depending upon country of performance.

CAUTION: Professional and amateur producers are hereby warned that UPROAR IN THE HOUSE is subject to a licensing fee. Publication of this play does not imply availability for performance. Both amateurs and professionals considering a production are strongly advised to apply to the appropriate agent before starting rehearsals, advertising, or booking a theatre. A licensing fee must be paid whether the title is presented for charity or gain and whether or not admission is charged.

The professional rights in this play are controlled by Samuel French Ltd, 52 Fitzroy Street, London, W1T 5JR

No one shall make any changes in this title for the purpose of production. No part of this book may be reproduced, stored in a retrieval system, or transmitted in any form, by any means, now known or yet to be invented, including mechanical, electronic, photocopying, recording, videotaping, or otherwise, without the prior written permission of the publisher. No one shall upload this title, or part of this title, to any social media websites.

The right of Anthony Marriott and Alistair Foot to be identified as authors of this work has been asserted in accordance with Section 77 of the Copyright, Designs and Patents Act 1988.

UPROAR IN THE HOUSE

This play was first presented by Brian Rix Enterprises, in association with Ernest Hecht, at the Garrick Theatre, London on 20th April, 1967 with the following cast:

CYRIL ALCOCK	Bill Treacher
MONICA JOHNSON	Anna Dawson
YVONNE WILBY	Wendy Padbury
MELANIE SINCLAIR	Elspet Gray
BERNARD LOCKWOOD	Leo Franklyn
NIGEL PITT	Brian Rix
SIR LINDSAY COOPER	Derek Farr
LADY COOPER	Helen Jessop
DAVID PROSSER	Dennis Ramsden
ANDREW GREY	Alan Tilvern
AUDREY GREY	Sheila Mercier
THE PHOTOGRAPHER	Andrew Sachs
ISABEL	Bernadette Gibson

Directed by WALLACE DOUGLAS

Designed by RHODA GRAY

It was subsequently presented by Talus Productions Ltd., in association with Ernest Hecht, at the Whitehall Theatre, London on 19th October, 1967, with the following cast:

CYRIL ALCOCK	John Louis Mansi
MONICA JOHNSON	Barbara Whatley
YVONNE WILBY	Patricia Franklin
MELANIE SINCLAIR	Joan Sims
BERNARD LOCKWOOD	Arthur English
NIGEL PITT	Nicholas Parsons
SIR LINDSAY COOPER	Geoffrey Sumner
LADY COOPER	Christine Russell
DAVID PROSSER	Peter Butterworth

ANDREW GREY	Anthony Howard
AUDREY GREY	Sheila Mercier
THE PHOTOGRAPHER	Bob Todd
ISABEL	Virginia Balfour

Directed by DENNIS RAMSDEN
Designed by RHODA GRAY

The action takes place in a Show House selected as House of the Year by "His and Hers" Magazine.

ACT ONE
 Scene One   A late afternoon in autumn
 Scene Two   Early evening

ACT TWO   Much later the same evening

PRODUCTION NOTE

How to succeed in farce without really trying? The straight answer is already suggested in this short sentence – don't try too hard. Don't allow any of your actors to approach "UPROAR IN THE HOUSE" with a 'funny hat' complex, determined to get a laugh almost before they have uttered a word of dialogue. Laughs they may well get as they make their entrance, but the really big character and situation laughs will evade them as the evening progresses. The basic plot of "UPROAR IN THE HOUSE" and its development in the early stages could really happen. Therefore, be real. Then, later on, as the fun develops quite naturally and the situations become more hilarious the players will reap the reward of almost continuous laughter because the audience are believing in what they see and yet the proceedings remain completely controlled by the discipline of the acting. Obviously pace is important but be careful to work up to it gradually, reaching full momentum from the discovery of the photographer hidden under the tree seat until the final curtain.

The set as designed for the London production may be difficult for some companies to reproduce and I have therefore devised a much simpler two-level design which still incorporates most of the business involved in the original production. The only tricky effect is the ball on the balustrade which jumps off into Alcock's hand each time he puts his foot on the step. This is worked by having a spring plunger down the centre of the balustrade and connected to a wire leading off-stage. When the wire is released on cue the plunger shoots up and the ball projected about four feet high.

DENNIS RAMSDEN

UPROAR IN THE HOUSE

ACT ONE

Scene 1

The curtain rises on the interior set to end all interior sets. It is the main living area of an extraordinary ultra-modern house - a house, indeed, that was built as the "His and Hers" Magazine House of the Year. Unfortunately, the year was 1962 and the house has never been sold since.

Through the vast picture windows, L, there are panoramic views of the South Downs, but you cannot have this sort of view and accessibility as well, which may be one of the reasons why this unique house still awaits its first owner.

U.C. is an open-tread spiral staircase which rises through the landing above like a submarine conning tower. The landing has on it four doors, reading from L to R: main bedroom door; bathroom door; first guest room door; and second guest room door. Underneath the master bedroom and bathroom and behind the staircase on the ground floor is the dining area. The entrance to this is gained U.L. via two open-tread steps.

Also in the alcove U.L. and opposite the dining area is the door leading to the kitchen. Behind the staircase is an enormous stained glass window depicting an abstract nude with a large eye looking out of it.

D.L. is the fully-glazed main door. U.R., also up a raised level in the centre of the room, is the door to the au pair's suite. This is a stable type door with separate top and bottom halves. In the facing wall between this and the dining area is a built-in television and stereo set. D.R. is the door to the nursery suite. U.R.C. there is, of all things, a tree growing to a height of at least seven feet. From the ceiling hang clusters of Danish light fittings; there may be more but there are certainly stalactites of them D.R., D.L. and U.C. over the staircase.

Hanging from the underside of the landing, in front of the dining area wall, is one of those large, suspended wicker chairs on two chains. Near it, U.R.C., is a large love seat which also acts as the surround for the tree which appears to grow out of the middle of it.

There is, however, quite a sizeable gap between the trunk of the tree and the surrounding enough for a small man to crouch inside. A slim small-bore central heating radiator runs the length of the window. Among other furnishings – all in the modern idiom – are two of those ghastly cone-shaped wicker chairs that tip up at the least provocation, and a low coffee table hewn out of an extremely heavy chunk of teak. Dust covers shroud the main chairs. By the panoramic window is a telephone with a long lead. The overall effect is like Heal's run wild. Although the set is fully furnished, it is only partially dressed – there are vertical blinds at the windows, for example, but no curtains. In the middle of the set, there are two open suitcases, a valise and a packing case with wood straw on the floor around it.

Standing sideways-on D.R., is a tall aluminium step ladder clearly marked "Lockwood's Maintenance Dept." The only other essential item is a red knob slightly larger than a cricket ball which surmounts the spiral staircase newel post if it had one as such. This knob matches a row of similar knobs spaced along the landing rail.

The set is deserted at first sight. Then the main door, D.L. opens to admit CYRIL ALCOCK. He is a small, slight man in his late thirties. His air of fatal resignation does not somehow match his lightness of foot. He is wearing working clothes topped by a somewhat overlarge donkey jacket bearing the word 'LOCKWOOD' in orange luminous letters on the back. He is trying to negotiate the doorway with a large pane of glass. He is suffering from a cold and as he gets to L.C., he starts the beginning of a big sneeze. He gets the glass down only just in time, completes his sneeze, blows his nose and picks the glass up again. He has just reached the entrance to the alcove U.L., when the central heating radiator by the window starts to emit a weird combination of knocking, tapping, and gurgling. He puts

Scene 1   UPROAR IN THE HOUSE

down the glass in great haste, leaps to his toolbag which is on
top of the packing case, and rummages for the right spanner.
He finds it and adjusts a nut on the radiator so that the knocking,
tapping, and gurgling subside with a final strangulated moan.
The job finishes to the accompaniment of another gigantic sneeze.
The radiator gurlges a short reply.

ALCOCK   (looking at it) Ta!   (He stuffs the spanner
                  in his pocket, picks up the glass and moves
                  rapidly into the kitchen.)

                  (There is a moment's pause, another – even
                  bigger – sneeze, followed by the shattering
                  of a window pane. ALCOCK emerges with
                  an expression of pained resignation and two
                  bits of glass and hurries out D.L.

                  Immediately, MISS JOHNSON enters from
                  the Nursery D.R. MONICA JOHNSON is
                  about 23, bespectacled, well-groomed but
                  not beautiful, and efficient but not over-
                  powering. She is carrying a large,
                  abstract reproduction which she is about
                  to hang over the door D.R. She looks at
                  the picture but cannot decide which is the
                  right way up. After looking at it both ways,
                  she decides that the first way was right and
                  climbs up the ladder with it. She is just
                  about to hang the picture from a protuberance
                  on the wall, when YVONNE WILBY rushes
                  in D.L. carrying a stack of modern square
                  saucepans of difference sizes. YVONNE
                  WILBY is about 16 and cocky with it. As
                  the office junior, she looks like a diminutive
                  mod with her pop art clothes and make-up
                  that is almost as clumsy as she is. As she
                  attempts to close the front door from behind
                  the pile of saucepans, she drops the lot and
                  lets out a shriek. MISS JOHNSON, startled
                  by the noise, almost drops the painting and
                  falls off the ladder.)

MISS JOHNSON   For heaven's sake, Yvonne, you nearly had
                  me off. Have you got two left hands or
                  something?

YVONNE   No, Miss Johnson, but my sister reckons her

boy friend has – and two right hands an'
all. (Her piercing laugh matches her
grating voice. She starts picking up the
saucepans.) Oh, sorry, Miss Johnson.
This is all a waste of time anyway. Old
Lockwood'll never sell a crazy place like
this. Look at that groovy staircase for a
start. If you came down that too fast, you
could screw yourself into the floor. (She
laughs, scuttles out U.L., and disappears
into the kitchen with all but one of the pans
which she has unwittingly left by the front
door.)

(Immediately, there is another loud clatter
from the kitchen. At the same time the front
door opens and ALCOCK comes in carrying
another sheet of glass. He steps into the
remaining saucepan and starts staggering
around trying to kick the saucepan off and
still maintain his balance with the glass.)

ALCOCK Oh... oh, gor blimey. I've stepped into something – something with a handle.

MISS JOHNSON (rushing down the steps to him) Mr. Alcock. Mr. Alcock. Mind that glass.

ALCOCK Get it off, get it off, Miss Johnson: it's me best dancing foot, me best dancing foot. (From behind the glass.) Get it off quick. I feel like a ruddy goldfish.

(MISS JOHNSON tugs at the saucepan as he
balances precariously on one leg. The
saucepan comes away suddenly with his shoe
inside it. He falls back on to the love seat,
just managing to save the glass. He lets
MISS JOHNSON hold the glass and starts to
nurse his foot which has the big toe protrud-
ing through a large hole in the sock.)

ALCOCK Oh, me metatarsus! What've I done to me metatarsus? Just when I needed me passo doble to be at its most spectacular, it'll be lopsided.

MISS JOHNSON	(trying to get his shoe out of the saucepan) What are you talking about, Mr. Alcock?
ALCOCK	The competition - dancing competition - southern area finals - Latin-American, I am - me and Miss Brown.
MISS JOHNSON	(giving him the shoe)　　Here you are - one sole bonne femme.
ALCOCK	Eh?
MISS JOHNSON	Never mind. I didn't know you went in for ballroom dancing.
ALCOCK	(sneezing)　　Innit marvellous? I got a cold as well. Yeah, me and my lady partner, Mavis Brown, we've been at it for years. Amateurs of course, not pros. We're quite well known round here: Alcock and Brown.
MISS JOHNSON	Alcock and Brown? I thought they were fliers?
ALCOCK	(putting his shoe on and picking up the glass)　　So were we until this happened. (He moves below MISS JOHNSON to U.L. of contemporary chair.)　　Who left that ruddy thing there, anyway?
MISS JOHNSON	Who do you think?
ALCOCK) MISS JOHNSON)	(together)　　Miss Wilby!
YVONNE	(scurrying out of the kitchen U.L.) Yeah? What's the matter? What have I done wrong now?
MISS JOHNSON	Oh, never mind. There's no time for messing about. Mr. Lockwood says we've got to sell this house today. By the way, have you fixed the upstairs ballcock, Mr. Alcock?
ALCOCK	Give us a chance. Anyway, I'm from General Maintenance - I'm not sanitary. I've never been sanitary.　　(He goes off talking to himself U.L. and limping slightly.)　　Fancy sending me up at a moment's notice to get the place ready when it's been empty for five

                    UPROAR IN THE HOUSE   ACT I

                    years. Everything's going wrong – the
                    plumbing – the glazing – electrics. I've
                    never seen anything like it.   (He is gone.)

YVONNE   'Ere, shall I take this <u>valliss</u> back down to
                    the van?

MISS JOHNSON   You can take the <u>valise</u> if it's empty.

YVONNE   (producing two toothbrushes)   It is, apart
                    from these toothbrushes.

MISS JOHNSON   They won't be needing them but you'd better
                    put them in the bathroom – makes it look
                    authentic.

YVONNE   Blimey, not up that corkscrew again. I'll
                    go in a minute.   (She puts the toothbrushes
                    in a piperack by the telephone.)

MISS JOHNSON   Get a move on. Mr. Lockwood will be here
                    before we've finished.

YVONNE   (picking up the valise and going towards the
                    door)   Not if he takes the short-cut like
                    us and ends up in that chicken farm. No
                    wonder they can't sell this way-out place –
                    it's so way out no one can't find it.   (She
                    starts to go out of the door.)

MISS JOHNSON   (calling)   Don't forget the French bread
                    and pyjamas.

YVONNE   (off)   Okay.

                    (MISS JOHNSON folds up the steps and
                    starts to go out with them into the Nursery
                    D.R. when the central heating system starts
                    its strange noises again.)

MISS JOHNSON   (shouting as she goes off)   Mr. Alcock!

                    (ALCOCK dashes out of the kitchen wielding
                    his spanner and starts to attack the radiator
                    with it.)

ALCOCK   Cor, stone me! I'll bet Harry Smith-Hampshire
                    never has trouble with his pipes. I'll never
                    get to the Locarno tonight.

                    (The telephone rings by his ear. He picks
                    it up.)

                    Hello?   I can't hear you..... I've got an

Scene 1 UPROAR IN THE HOUSE

>airlock in me flow pipe and I can't find me nipple. This is Cyril Alcock speaking.... That's right, this is the Show House.... Hold on... (Shouts.) Miss Johnson!
>
>(MISS JOHNSON comes hurrying in D.R.)
>
>It's Post Office Engineers - they want to test you to see if you're normal!

MISS JOHNSON (reacts then takes the phone) Thank you very much... Sorry, we only arrived half an hour ago....

>(ALCOCK gives the radiator a final turn and the noise subsides.)
>
>Oh, that noise! ... I'm sorry, what did you say? .... Well, it's working all right now...
>
>(ALCOCK hurries into the kitchen U.L.)
>
>Thank you for getting the phone put in at such short notice.... By the way, who do we have to speak to about getting it taken out? .... The telephone, of course.
>
>(The door chimes ring out, jam and keep on ringing.)
>
>Mr. Alcock!
>
>(ALCOCK rushes out from U.L.)
>
>(To ALCOCK.) There's somebody at the door. (Into phone.) Yes, I know the phone's only just been put in but we may only want it for twenty four hours... We'll write to you. (She puts down the phone.)
>
>(ALCOCK opens the door. He kicks the door jamb and the chimes stop. MISS JOHNSON moves to R. and tidies suitcases below T.V. set. YVONNE comes in carrying new pyjamas in cellophane wrappers, a nightdress and two long loaves of french bread.)

YVONNE I locked meself out. (Crosses below ALCOCK and turns to him.) 'Ere, what's the matter with them chimes?

ALCOCK	I dunno. They're up the spout, like everything else in this house.
YVONNE	You speak for yourself, cheeky! (She crosses to U.S. of tree seat.)
	(ALCOCK hurries back to the kitchen.)
	It ain't half getting cold and misty out there. (She puts the loaves on the love seat and holds up the gaudy pyjamas.) 'Ere, these are real gear, aren't they? I can't see our Mr. Pitt wearing them. He's a right square Sales Manager, he is.
MISS JOHNSON	He won't have to, Yvonne. I've told you before they're only for the sake of appearances.
YVONNE	(holding up the diaphanous nightdress) Look at that! What my dad calls a News of the World nightie.
MISS JOHNSON	News of the World?
YVONNE	Yeah. Everything exposed on a Sunday morning. (She laughs.) You wanna ask old Lockwood to let you have this when it's all over. It'd send your boyfriend mad.
MISS JOHNSON	I haven't got a boyfriend.
YVONNE	You soon would have if you wore one of these. (She lays the nightdress over the love seat.)
MISS JOHNSON	Just take the bread to the kitchen and the night things upstairs. I'll put the children's photographs out.
YVONNE	(going out U.L. with the bread) Whose kids are they, anyway?
MISS JOHNSON	(putting a large photograph of three children on a side table U.C.) I don't know. They're only borrowed like the rest of it.
	(MISS JOHNSON returns C. and has just loaded herself up with an armful of tinned food from the suitcase when the door chimes ring out, jam, and go on ringing.)

Scene 1 UPROAR IN THE HOUSE 9

YVONNE (running in from U.L.) Blimey, that's done it. Old Lockwood's here already. I told you we had to get a move on.

MISS JOHNSON Answer it then – I've got an armful. (She disappears into the kitchen.)

(YVONNE clatters down to the door. She kicks the door jamb with her foot, reacts in pain, and the chiming stops. She opens the door. Outside stands MELANIE SINCLAIR. She is an extremely attractive but little known actress in her late twenties. She is intelligent, with a keen sense of fun, if a bit inclined to "camp it up".)

MELANIE Good evening. I'm Melanie Sinclair.

YVONNE Oh, come in, Miss. (She shuts the door.)

MELANIE (crossing to C. and putting make-up box on tree seat) I don't know whether I've come to the right place. I just finished up in a chicken farm. Does a Mr. Lockwood live here?

YVONEE Nobody don't live here. But this is his house all right – and he wishes it wasn't. You'd better come in. He'll be here in a minute and we haven't finished unpacking. (She limps towards the kitchen.)

(MELANIE follows into the room. At the same time, ALCOCK comes limping out of the kitchen carrying a ballcock complete with armature. YVONNE and ALCOCK pass each other, both limping heavily, but take no notice.)

ALCOCK (as he passes MELANIE) Afternoon. (He gives an enormous sneeze.)

MELANIE Bless you.

(ALCOCK reaches the spiral staircase and plants his foot firmly on the bottom step. The red ball on the newell post pops like a clay pigeon into the air and lands in his free hand.)

ALCOCK (amazed and standing like a king holding

		the orb and screptre) Did you see that? It jumped clean off.
MELANIE		Well, you've got the orb and sceptre: all you need now is a crown and you're set for the Old Vic.
ALCOCK		(putting the red ball back on the 'Newell Post') I could do with some of that with a cold like mine. This place is falling apart at the seams, falling apart at the seams. (He goes up the staircase and disappears into the bathroom.)
		(At the same time, MISS JOHNSON comes hurrying out of the kitchen. She and MELANIE SINCLAIR meet C.)
MISS JOHNSON		Ah, you must be Miss Sinclair, our actress.
MELANIE		That's right. Unknown star of stage, screen and television.
MISS JOHNSON		I'm Monica Johnson – Mr. Lockwood's secretary. I spoke to your agent last night.
MELANIE.		Bully for you. It's more than I've been able to do for weeks.
MISS JOHNSON		But if you haven't spoken to him, do you know what we want?
MELANIE		I got a vague message. Something about playing the wife of a young executive.
MISS JOHNSON		That's right. (Crossing and shutting a suitcase.) Sorry everything's so chaotic. We're trying to make the place look lived-in for the clients.
MELANIE		By the way, is this being filmed for television or the cinema?
MISS JOHNSON		(furiously sticking artificial flowers into a window box by the door D.L.,) It's not being filmed for anything this afternoon. It was on both when it was chosen as the House of the Year, but that was five years ago. And a fat lot of good it did us.
MELANIE		(sitting D.S. of tree seat) Don't tell me my agent's given me the wrong day again?

Scene 1   UPROAR IN THE HOUSE

MISS JOHNSON	No, it's the right day. Mr. Lockwood and Mr. Pitt should be here any time. You're going to be Mr. Pitt's wife, of course.
MELANIE	Not Rodney Pitt? I was at The Intimate with him.
MISS JOHNSON	I beg your pardon?
MELANIE	The Intimate, Palmer's Green. I think it was "Waters of the Moon".
	(The bathroom door opens and ALCOCK comes out.)
ALCOCK	Right. I've fixed the ballcock. (Coming down stairs.) And I've done the lock as well – it was sticking.
MISS JOHNSON	Thanks. See to that loose switch in the main bedroom, will you?
ALCOCK	(pausing and then going back up the stairs towards the master bedroom) Right-ho.
MISS JOHNSON	No, Miss Sinclair, it wasn't Rodney Pitt I was talking about. Our Mr. Pitt is Nigel. Yvonne!
MELANIE	Nigel? I don't think I've ever played with him.
MISS JOHNSON	No, and I don't think anyone else has. (She laughs nervously.)
	(YVONNE enters.)
	Oh, dear. (Shouts.) Yvonne, find somewhere to put those suitcases.
YVONNE	Where am I supposed to put 'em?
MISS JOHNSON	Anywhere. In the garage – just get rid of them.
YVONNE	(going off U.L. with empty suitcases) Cor, what a drag. All this running around for just half an hour.
MISS JOHNSON	(taking dust sheet off contemporary chair and putting it in packing case L.C.) I'm sorry. You were saying?

MELANIE		This Nigel Pitt. Is he very experienced?
MISS JOHNSON		I've never had a chance to find out. He's more interested in politics than anything else.
MELANIE		I see – another Andrew Faulds?
MISS JOHNSON		Hardly. Mr. Pitt's Conservative – in more ways than one. He's hoping to be adopted as the candidate for this constituency. In fact, he's been attending the final selection committee today.
MELANIE		Good for him.
MISS JOHNSON		(rushing around taking dust covers off chairs and putting them in one of the cases) So, of course, he doesn't know anything about these arrangements. At least, he will do now because he'll have been back to the office before being sent out here. But he didn't before that because it hadn't happened before he went.
MELANIE		(sending her up) I'm glad you told me – otherwise I might have gone before he came.

(YVONNE comes in from the kitchen.)

MISS JOHNSON It's all quite straighforward. Yvonne, for heaven's sake take those pyjamas and nightdress upstairs to the master bedroom for Mr. Pitt and Miss Sinclair.

(YVONNE moves to staircase but is stopped by MELANIE.)

MELANIE Hey, wait a minute, wait a minute. Pyjamas and nightdress? What's going on here? Just what sort of films do your company make?

YVONNE (taking pyjamas and nightdress and starting up staircase) Films? We don't make films, miss, we build and sell houses. Lockwood's Luxury Homesteads, that's us. (She steps on the bottom step, the ball shoots up in the air and MELANIE manages to catch it.) I never done it, Miss

Scene 1 UPROAR IN THE HOUSE

Johnson, I never done it - it done itself.

(Before anybody has time to say anything else, the front door chimes ring, jam and go on ringing.)

MISS JOHNSON Now we're for it. Answer the door. I'll put this on again.

(She takes the ball from MELANIE and screws it back on again as YVONNE rushes D.R. taking no notice of MELANIE.)

MELANIE (over) But my agent said there was a part here in a commercial. Is there one or isn't there?

(YVONNE drops pyjamas etc. in armchair U.C.)

YVONNE (over: at the same time) Oh dear, oh dear, I shall have one of me queer turns after all this, I know I will. (She kicks the door jamb, the chimes stop, she reacts in pain again and opens the door.) Good afternoon, Mr. Lockwood, sir. (She stands there one-legged like a mini-stork.)

LOCKWOOD (crossing below YVONNE then turning) What's the matter with you, then? Got one suspender shorter than the other? I don't s'pose you've noticed, but that bell needs fixing. Where's Pitt? Is Pitt here yet?

(LOCKWOOD stumps in and crosses to C. He is elderly but extremely active. He started with two men and a ladder and has ended up with a minor building empire. But his rough, direct manner has never changed. This coarse aggressiveness contrasts somewhat with his clothes because he is well turned out. He carries an ash walking stick in one hand and an ornate birdcage, with a stuffed bird in it, in the other.)

MISS JOHNSON Not yet, Mr. Lockwood, but he must be on his way.

LOCKWOOD He'd better be - or I'll have him on his

	way for good. It's getting misty outside. I took the short cut and finished up in that damned chicken farm again: up to me neck in muck and pullets. (He peers at MELANIE.) Hello, hello, hello. Who are you, then? Are you from Accounts, Personnel or Advertising?
MELANIE	(sitting left end of tree seat) Neither.
LOCKWOOD	You can't have neither of three. I may have left school when I was eleven but at least I know that. If your English grammar's that bad, you <u>must</u> be from Advertising.
MELANIE	I am not from Advertising, <u>neither</u> am I from one of the other two.
LOCKWOOD	That's better. At least I've learned you something. What am I standing here with this birdcage for? Oh yes, that's right. I brought it to tart this place up a bit. I've been trying to get rid of it ever since the wife gave it to me for Christmas. If there's one thing a man of my age doesn't need, it's a stuffed bird. (He gives it to MISS JOHNSON.) Here you are, go and hang it up in the Nursery.
	(As MISS JOHNSON goes out D.R., LOCKWOOD turns to MELANIE.)
	Who did you say you were?
MELANIE	I didn't. I was sent here by the Simmonds Theatrical Agency, and I wish somebody would tell me what's going on.
LOCKWOOD	You're our tame actress, are you? Very nice, too. I wish I was a couple of years younger. Yes, I recognise you now. I've seen you on the telly, haven't I? Rolling around in the long grass with a Nux bar or something fruity.
MELANIE	Well, it's the choc-bars that pay for the Chekhov.
LOCKWOOD	And it's my semis, sixteen to an acre, that have paid for this nancy nightmare.

MELANIE		You actually build sixteen houses to the acre?
LOCKWOOD		Yes, shocking waste of space, isn't it? But it's those daft council bye-laws. 'Course, I never wanted to build this house in the first place. But my Chief Architect sucked up to the Board, talked 'em into it and then scarpered to West Africa to build gold-plated bathrooms for some damned democratic despot.
MELANIE		You can't have a democratic despot – it's a contradiction in terms.
LOCKWOOD		Well, there's no need to be rude about it. I may be a bit of a rough diamond, but I'm never rude to anyone. (He turns to YVONNE, who is still D.L.) Don't just stand there gawping, you daft idiot, get this place tidied up.
YVONNE		(scuttling to packing case) Yes, sir. Yes, sir. I was just going to do it, sir. (She picks up the packing case after a struggle and staggers into the kitchen with it.)
LOCKWOOD		(turning to MELANIE as YVONNE wheels into the kitchen) Right. You know what you're being paid to do and who you're going to do it with, don't you?
MELANIE		No, I don't – but I hope it's not what it sounds like.
		(ALCOCK comes out of the master bedroom and hurries down the stairs. As he gets to the bottom step he treads gingerly, looking at the red ball. It stays where it is. He has just left the stairs, when the ball flies off on its own accord.)
ALCOCK		(holding the ball) It did it again. It did it again. I'm not a ball-boy, you know.
LOCKWOOD		Then get off the court!
		(ALCOCK sticks the ball back on and hurries out U.L.)

	(He crosses to C.) Now you know what it's all about so that's settled you.
MELANIE	(rising to LOCKWOOD) I don't know what it's all about and it's far from settled as far as I'm concerned.
LOCKWOOD	You and Pitt should make a right pair – you're just as stubborn as he is. (He crosses below MELANIE and circles round tree to R. of her.) Look at this place. Will you look at it? I've had twenty-four thousand quid tied up in it for five years. And all I've had out of it is a load of rubbish in His and Hers magazine. (He goes all posh.) This avant garde home combines the subtle use of space and levels to capture the ever-changing moods of modern living. (His own voice.) Whatever that means.
MELANIE	It means it's a modern white elephant.
LOCKWOOD	You're telling me. And the longer it stays on the market, the more impssible it becomes. It's like an unmarried Scoutmaster of fifty – everybody thinks there's something wrong with it.
MELANIE	And is there?
LOCKWOOD	Well, there's something wrong with this place all right. It's impossible to live in it – nothing but stairs. That's why I've decided the only way to sell it is to have somebody living in it.
MELANIE	You're going to let it to a family temporarily?
LOCKWOOD	What! And have this lovely, desirable house mucked about by a lot of grubby hands? Not damn likely. I'm not going to <u>have</u> it occupied. I'm just going to make it <u>look</u> as if it's occupied.
MELANIE	It sounds rather like false pretences to me.
LOCKWOOD	False pretences? How can it be false pretences if it's occupied by my own Sales Manager? He's spent five years <u>not</u>

Scene 1 UPROAR IN THE HOUSE 17

>   selling it so now he can damned well start.
>   There's only one trouble: he's not married.
>   That's where you come in.
>
> MELANIE   I beg your pardon? Are you seriously
>   suggesting I should live alone in this house
>   with your Sales Manager?
>
> LOCKWOOD   Not live with him - just act the part. And
>   you've only got to do that for half an hour
>   while Sir Lindsay and Lady Cooper have a
>   butcher's.
>
> MELANIE   (crossing to tree seat and picking up make-
>   up box)   That's all it is? I'm afraid
>   you've picked the wrong girl. I only came
>   here because I thought it was a high-class
>   commercial.
>
> LOCKWOOD   That's just what it is. And you're being
>   well paid for it. I'll bet it's a damn sight
>   more than you get for prancing around
>   fields, nibbling chocolate bars. (He does
>   the Cadbury's Flake routine.)   Go on -
>   spoil yourself.   Treat yourself to sixpence
>   worth of heaven.   (He blows a raspberry.)
>
> MELANIE   (sitting on tree seat)   You do it better
>   than I do.
>
> LOCKWOOD   Well, I've had more experience. And that's
>   not all. If you pull the deal off and Sir
>   Lindsay decides to buy, I'll pitt Split's
>   commission - spit Pitt's commi - I'll give
>   you half his money.
>
>   (MISS JOHNSON runs in D.R. holding a
>   bath brush.)
>
>   Where d'you think you're going?
>
> MISS JOHNSON   (pointing with the bath brush) Upstairs,
>   sir.   (She goes upstairs, holding the
>   red ball down as she does so, and disappears
>   into the bathroom.)
>
>   (At the same time ALCOCK comes out U.L.
>   carrying his toolbag.)
>
> LOCKWOOD   (to ALCOCK)   And where the hell d'you

		think you're going?
ALCOCK		I'm knocking off, unless you want me on time-and-a – ah...ah...ah...attishoo! – half.
LOCKWOOD		No, I don't. This place has cost me enough already.
ALCOCK		Right. I'm going to have a couple of goes with Miss Brown before we get on the floor. (He goes out.)
		(As ALCOCK goes out LOCKWOOD turns and notices the night things for the first time.)
LOCKWOOD		What a common workman! Good God, what're those pyjamas doing there? Miss Wilby!
YVONNE		(scuttling in U.L.) Yes, sir. Yes, sir. Yes, sir.
LOCKWOOD		Where the hell have those pyjamas come from?
YVONNE		Marks and Spencers, sir. We bought them out of Petty Cash.
LOCKWOOD		I don't mean that. I mean why are they there?
YVONNE		'Cos every time I try to take them upstairs I get interfered with.
LOCKWOOD.		There must be an answer to that. Don't just stand there, take them up now before the Coopers get here.
YVONNE		Yes, sir. Yes, sir. (She picks up the pyjamas and nightdress and runs up the stairs. The red ball jumps off but she does not notice.)
MELANIE		Don't let me interrupt anything, Mr. Lockwood, but do you mind if I make my position clear?
LOCKWOOD		(catching the ball and looking at the tree) What's this – a windfall? (He puts the ball down on the contemporary chair L.C.)

MELANIE		I was trying to say –
LOCKWOOD		What the devil's happened to Pitt?

(The front chimes ring, jam, and go on chiming.)

Miss Wilby! Front door!

(YVONNE, nearly at the top of the stairs, is caught undecided. Should she answer the door? Or get rid of the pyjamas? The door wins. She rushes down stairs, throws the nightwear back on the tree-seat and crosses to the door.)

(At the same time) Now then, if this is the Coopers, it's up to you. Tell 'em your old man's out and start showing 'em round. Cooper knows me. If he sees me here, he'll smell a rat. I'm off.

(YVONNE kicks the door jamb and stops the chimes.)

MELANIE	But I haven't been round the house myself. I don't know where anything is.
LOCKWOOD	(turning as bell stops) Miss Wilby! What the hell are you doing?
YVONNE	Opening the door, sir, like you said.
LOCKWOOD	Don't be such a damned idiot. You're not supposed to be here. Cooper knows you. He saw you at the office.
YVONNE	It's not him, sir, it's Mr. Pitt – our Mr. Pitt!
LOCKWOOD	Then don't just stand there – let him in, let him in!
YVONNE	Yes, sir. Yes, sir. (She opens the door.)

(PITT sweeps in. He is smartly dressed in the best British manner. He is good looking and certainly a most eligible bachelor. But he is not the typical sales manager. Indeed, his normal role is to bring a little class and tone to the

	UPROAR IN THE HOUSE ACT I
	proceedings. At the present moment he is highly elated and even more extrovert than usual.)
PITT	Vote Pitt, P - I - double T, Pitt - Conservative.
	(PITT picks YVONNE up in his arms and plants a kiss upon her cheek.)
YVONNE	Oh, Mr. Pitt. Mr. Pitt!
PITT	Yvonne, you may congratulate me. I have just been adopted as your Parliamentary candidate.
LOCKWOOD	Well, well, well. Benjamin Disraeli's come home at last. Put her down, man. The baby kissing comes later.
	(PITT drops YVONNE heavily. She squeals and hurries out U.L.)
PITT	Oh, good gracious, I didn't realise you were here, Mr. Lockwood. I didn't see your car.
LOCKWOOD	'Course not. I put it round the back out of sight. Always have done - ever since I got married. What the wife doesn't see, her heart doesn't grieve for.
PITT	The office told me you've found someone to con into - (He sees MELANIE.) - to conduct round this unique property. (He crosses to MELANIE.)
	(MELANIE rises.)
	How do you do, madam. I'm so sorry I wasn't here when you arrived.
LOCKWOOD	Don't be a damn fool, man. That's not the customer - that's your wife.
PITT	Oh, how do you do. MY WHAT??
MELANIE	There's no need to look so surprised. You'd be amazed at the things I can do with a couple of Oxo cubes.
MISS JOHNSON	(with great banging from the bathroom)

	Help! Help! I'm locked in the bathroom.
LOCKWOOD	(shouts) Miss Wilby!
YVONNE	(rushing back) Yes, sir. Yes, sir. Yes, sir.
LOCKWOOD	Miss Bathson's locked in the john. I mean Miss Johnson's locked in the bath. Get her out - get her out.
	(YVONNE runs upstairs.)
	Now look here, Pitt, there's no time to waste. The Coopers could be here at any moment.
PITT	The Coopers?
LOCKWOOD	Sir Lindsay Cooper, you great ignorant parliamentary candidate. He wants to buy a house that's different, so you'd better sell him this one.
	(YVONNE forces open the bathroom door and hurtles inside.
	Miss Johnson, what've you been doing in the bathroom all this time?
MISS JOHNSON	(emerging) Trying to get out, sir. There's something the matter with the lock - it keeps sticking.
LOCKWOOD	Then for God's sake unstick it. Get some oil from somewhere.
MISS JOHNSON	I'll look in the garage, Mr. Lockwood. (She descends the stairs with YVONNE and goes out U.L. with her.)
LOCKWOOD	Now look here, Pitt, you can pull this off as long as Sir Lindsay don't find out how many people have turned it down before. That's why I want it occupied right now by a typical, happy married couple. No, no, that's not right. If they were typical, they wouldn't be happy. Anyway, you know what I mean.
MELANIE	(putting her arm round PITT) We'll be very happy, won't we, darling?

PITT		(horrified and removing her arm) Mr. Lockwood, you don't mean - you're not suggesting -
LOCKWOOD		I am.
PITT		I am absolutely speechless - words fail me.
LOCKWOOD		That's a bloody change.

(During the following speech LOCKWOOD's jaw sags lower and lower as he completely loses track of what is being said.)

PITT   Accustomed as I am, after all these years, to your unusual methods of management, I have never, but never, heard of any company executive being placed in such an untenable position. (He moves down stage, circling round to behind contemporary chair.) As you are aware, sir, I have today had the honour to be adopted as Conservative parliamentary candidate for this constituency - a constituency which has suffered in the past from a Member whose private moral behaviour has led not only himself but his party, his constituency and his innocent supporters into a maelstrom of political denigration.

LOCKWOOD   Oh, cor blimey.

PITT   Indeed, sir, I have no doubt whatsoever that my selection this afternoon by Sir Norman Spens and the members of the adoption committee was due almost entirely to the fact that my integrity and unblemished reputation as a bachelor were beyond dispute. Indeed, Sir Norman Spens himself commented upon it. In the circumstances, I feel it is quite impossible for me to condone any situation which might compromise me and thereby flagrantly disregard the large measure of trust which has been placed in me by my party.

(MELANIE and LOCKWOOD applaud rapidly and enthusiastically.)

LOCKWOOD   Well, either you do it or you're fired.

Scene 1 UPROAR IN THE HOUSE 23

PITT
In that case, I am left with no alternative but to tender my resignation as Group Sales Manager for Lockwood's Luxury Homesteads.

LOCKWOOD
Well, you can stuff your resignation – in your ballot box. If you go it'll be because I've given you the bullet. And I might as well warn you I'm not going to carry the can for any ugly rumours that might reach the shell-like virginal ears of Sir Norman Whatsit and his committee.

PITT
(breaking round to R. of chair) But – but – but this is absolutely monstrous! It's blackmail!

MELANIE
Mr. Lockwood, are you trying to coerce my husband?

(MISS JOHNSON comes in U.L. carrying an oil can, goes up the stairs and into the bathroom, shutting the door behind her, without the others noticing.)

LOCKWOOD
No, I'm putting the screws on him.
(He forces PITT to sit in chair and on to ball.) And I'm doing him a favour as well. If he wants to get into Parliament – and I'm not saying it would be bad for my firm if he did – then he needs me to pay his salary while he's doing it. Just as much as I need him to sell this house now. (He crosses to door D.L.) Now you two had better get together and sort yourselves out before the Coopers get here. Don't forget, you're supposed to have lived here, man and wife, for several years, so you should be at the bickering stage by now.

(The door chimes sound and stick. LOCKWOOD peeps through the venetian blind.)

Good God, they're here already!

PITT
They're here already!

LOCKWOOD
(shouts) Miss Wilby!

YVONNE
(scuttling in U.L., she rushes to the door,

	kicks the jamb and stops the chimes) Yes, sir. Yes, sir. Yes, sir.
LOCKWOOD	We're off. Where's Miss Johnson?
YVONNE	In the garage getting some oil for the loo, sir.
LOCKWOOD	Come on.
	(YVONNE goes out to the kitchen.)
	We'll pick her up on the way out. (He turns by the kitchen door.) And don't forget, Pitt, if this deal falls through, you may stand for Parliament – but I won't bloody well stand for you. (He hurries out U.L.)
PITT	(crossing to C. with MELANIE) What has he let me in for this time? If this ever gets out, my political career will be ruined before it's even started.
MELANIE	Never mind your political career. This could ruin my marriage.
PITT	Marriage? You're not married, are you? My God, I'm committing adultery. Whatever will the Primrose League say?
MELANIE	I'm not married yet, but I am engaged.
PITT	Thank goodness it's only that.
MELANIE	To a solicitor.
PITT	(aghast) To a solicitor!
	(The door chimes ring and stick. Copying Yvonne, PITT rushes D.R. and kicks the door jamb. He suddenly realises MELANIE has still got her coat on.)
	Oh, my God. Coat!
	(He grabs the coat from her, dashes to the Nursery and flings the coat inside. He is halfway back when she sees his coat.)
MELANIE	Coat!
	(She helps him off with his coat. Comedy

Scene 1 UPROAR IN THE HOUSE

business with the ball stuck up the sleeve, etc. The door chimes sound and stick again. PITT rushes D.R., kicks the door jamb, rushes back to the Nursery, taking his coat off at the same time, and flings it inside. MELANIE picks up the pyjamas and hurls them into the gap between the seat and the tree. She "reclines" on the tree seat. The door chimes sound and stick.)

PITT (rushing to the door) I'm coming. I'm coming. I'll never forgive Lockwood for this - never, never, never! (He kicks the door jamb, the chimes stop, and he opens the door, all charm.) Do come in.

(As SIR LINDSAY and LADY COOPER enter.)

I do hope we haven't kept you waiting.

(SIR LINDSAY is between fifty and sixty, smooth and bland if a little detached. LADY COOPER is in her mid-thirties, poised and elegant but there is something diffident about her manner.)

SIR LINDSAY Not at all, Mr. Pitt. (He sees MELANIE and crosses to her.) And Mrs. Pitt. How nice to meet you, my dear. It is Mrs. Pitt, isn't it?

PITT Yes, this is my wife, er - (He suddenly realises that he does not know her name.) - my wife, er -

MELANIE) (together) Melanie.
PITT) Barbara.

SIR LINDSAY I beg your pardon? What was that?

PITT Melanie.

MELANIE Barbara.

SIR LINDSAY I see.

PITT That's what's on her birth certificate, of course, but we actually call her - (He looks at MELANIE.) Bar - bar

	(MELANIE shakes her head.)
	– we actually call her Melanie.
SIR LINDSAY	What a pretty name, my dear. Now may I introduce you to –
PITT	Lady Cooper. Of course. Delighted to make your acquaintance. I'm sure I've seen your picture in The Horse and Hound.
LADY COOPER	Well, I hope you appreciated my seat.
PITT	I don't think I noticed that.
SIR LINDSAY	I'm afraid we're a bit early. It's getting rather foggy out and we have an engagement tonight, so we thought we'd make the trip while we could. I do hope it's not inconveniencing you.
MELANIE	Oh no, Sir Lindsay. You couldn't have come at a better time – could they, darling?
PITT	No, no, you couldn't have come at a better time. The family's away and we're here just waiting to show you round – all on our own.
	(MELANIE rises to below tree seat.)
LADY COOPER	(crossing to MELANIE) Do you run this place without help, Mrs. Pitt?
	(YVONNE pokes her head round the kitchen door and gapes into the room. PITT spots her and frantically waves her to go.)
MELANIE	(over) Yes, quite on my own. Not that it's difficult to get help round here. It's just that I adore housework.
	(SIR LINDSAY notices PITT's antics just as YVONNE disappears.)
SIR LINDSAY	Is anything the matter?
PITT	(converting his waving arm into definite arm exercises) No, just doing my arm exercises. I've had this trouble – what they call a frozen shoulder – and the specialist told me last week to do this –

	(He does more exercises.) – every now and again.
SIR LINDSAY	How very interesting. I suffer from a bit of muscular trouble, too. Gets me in the rifle shoulder. Nobody seems to do any good. Perhaps your chap could help. What's his name?
PITT	What's his name? His name! Well, er, he's a Harley Street man but it's such a long time since I visited him, I can't remember.
SIR LINDSAY	But surely you just said you visited him last week.
PITT	Yes, yes, I did. But he wasn't there, you see; I saw his partner.
SIR LINDSAY	Well, what's his name?
PITT	What, him or his partner?
SIR LINDSAY	Either.
PITT	Well, er – er –
MELANIE	Dr. Brown.
PITT	That's right, Dr. Brown. And his partner's name is – is –
MELANIE	(sitting on tree seat) Rothenstein.
PITT	Yes, Rothenstein.
SIR LINDSAY	Not William Rothenstein?
PITT	Yes, that's right, William Rothenstein.
SIR LINDSAY	Funn. Didn't know he was orthopaedic. He did me for gallstones.
PITT	Ah, well, they reckon it starts with gall-stones – and this is the latest treatment for gallstones – keeps them on the move. (Crossing below towards U.C.) I'm sure you'd like to see round the house straight away as you're short of time and it's getting foggy.
MELANIE	Yes, we'd better make the best of it before

	the children get home.
PITT	The children? Oh, yes, the children. (He starts ushering them towards the staircase.) Yes, they'll be back from school soon – won't they? Shall I lead the way? (He steps on the tread, the ball flies off and he catches it.) Good gracious!
SIR LINDSAY	Well held, sir!
PITT	(looking at the ball in his hand) Alas, poor Yorick, I knew him well. I'll get that fixed, of course; I've been meaning to do it for ages. (He puts the ball down.) Yes, this is the only peaceful part of the day when Bar – when Melanie and I are quite alone.
	(Violent banging from the bathroom.)
MISS JOHNSON	(muffled) Help! Help! I'm locked in again.
PITT	(aghast) Miss Johnson! She wasn't in the garage after all.
SIR LINDSAY	What did you say, old chap?
PITT	That's Miss – Johansenn, our au pair, you know. I thought she was doing something in the garage, but she must've been doing it in the bathroom, instead.
LADY COOPER	You do have an au pair, Mrs. Pitt? I thought you said you didn't have any help?
MELANIE	Au pairs are no help, are they? Take this one – Helga. Every time she goes to the bathroom, Nigel has to help her.
SIR LINDSAY	Help her?
PITT	Help her in the bathroom when she gets stuck – the door gets stuck. She's only just come over here, you see. She doesn't really understand our way of life.
MELANIE	Or our locks.
SIR LINDAY	Doesn't speak much English, I suppose?

Scene 1 UPROAR IN THE HOUSE

PITT	Practically none. That's why she's here – to learn English.
MISS JOHNSON	Mr. Pitt! Mr. Pitt! I'm incarcerated in this wretched bathroom again. Would you please come.
PITT	(rushing upstairs) All right, Miss Johansenn. I'm coming. (Precisely, as if to a foreigner, outside door.) Please do not exhaust yourself by saying another word in English – particularly as our visitors, Sir Lindsay and Lady Cooper, have just arrived here.
MISS JOHNSON	Heavens, they're not, are they?
PITT	Shut up – I mean stand back, Miss Johansenn. I'm going to force the door open.
	(SIR LINDSAY, LADY COOPER and MELANIE come up the stairs on to the landing.)
SIR LINDSAY	Want any help, old chap?
PITT	No, thanks, no. Leave her to me; I've got the knack. (He manages to force the door open.)
	(MISS JOHNSON comes hurrying out.)
MISS JOHNSON	All that time fiddling and –
PITT	(cutting in hastily) Don't worry, Miss Johansenn –
MISS JOHNSON	Johansenn?
PITT	Yes, you, Miss Johansenn. We quite understand that coming from Sweden you find – (Pointedly.) – everything is different here now.
MISS JOHNSON	Oh – er – oui – ya – mmmm. (She gives up her attempt to find the appropriate word and nods in what she thinks is a Swedish manner.)
PITT	But you're still the best au pair we've ever had and you're picking things up very quickly, aren't you?

MISS JOHNSON	Oh – er – oui – ya – mmmm.
MELANIE	(pointedly) Helga, this is Sir Lindsay and Lady Cooper, Helga, of whom you have heard Mr. Pitt and I speak. They are interested in buying our lovely house.
MISS JOHNSON	(crossing to between SIR LINDSAY and LADY COOPER, in severely fractured English) Oh, yes – is a lovely house. Is why so many peoples are coming to see and wanting to buy, yes?
SIR LINDSAY	(shouting as if to the deaf) I am not surprised, Miss Johansenn. It is a very nice house – what we have seen of it so far.
MISS JOHNSON	Oh, ya. I have most happy been here for a long times.
	(During this dialogue, YVONNE comes in from the kitchen U.L., looking for MISS JOHNSON again. She hears the voices and looks up. Once again, PITT sees her out of the corner of his eye. He gesticulates for her to leave, which she does hastily. Again, SIR LINDSAY turns and PITT has to convert his gestures into arm exercises.)
SIR LINDSAY	Gallstones on the move again, old chap?
PITT	It's nothing – nothing at all – just a twinge. Shall we have a look at the bedrooms first now we're up here, Lady Cooper?
LADY COOPER	You lead the way, Mr. Pitt.
PITT	It's all right, Helga, we shan't be needing you. You can go down to the kitchen and get the children's tea ready.
MISS JOHNSON	Ze tea for ze children?
PITT	Yes. And whatever you do, get rid of that little bundle of rubbish outside the back door.
MISS JOHNSON	Little bundle of – ? Oh, yes – ja – mmmm.
PITT	This is the master bedroom. (Going into room above U.L. with the others following.)

Scene 1   UPROAR IN THE HOUSE   31

> As you can see, it has fully fitted wardrobes and vanitory unit and, of course, its southerly aspect does give it the maximum amount of sunshine during the hours of daylight.
>
> (The door closes. MISS JOHNSON comes downstairs and meets YVONNE, who scuttles in from the kitchen.)

YVONNE Quick, Miss Johnson. Mr. Lockwood's waiting for you at the end of the drive and he's going potty.

MISS JOHNSON (starting in broken English) So sorry I am. (Reverting to normal.) I mean I can't come now. They know I'm here and they think I'm an au pair.

YVONNE Pair of what?

MISS JOHNSON They think I'm a Swede.

YVONNE Eh? But what'll I tell old Lockwood?

MISS JOHNSON Tell him I'll come back in the van - look out, here they come.

> (The master bedroom door opens. PITT comes out first, followed by SIR LINDSAY then LADY COOPER and MELANIE.)

SIR LINDSAY (off) You lead the way, old chap.

PITT Next door, of course, we have the b-a-a-a- (He goes into a strangulated cry as he sees YVONNE and starts his arm exercises again.)

> (YVONNE scurries out U.L. followed by MISS JOHNSON.)

Sorry, just another twinge.

SIR LINDSAY Are you sure Rothenstein's made the correct diagnosis?

PITT Oh yes, I have complete confidence in him, as I told him - as I told his partner - only last week.

LADY COOPER (coming out of bedroom) What a charming

	room. Tell me, Mrs. Pitt, how does one know which is one's side of the circular bed?
MELANIE	One doesn't: that's half the fun, isn't it, Nigel?
PITT	Oh, yes. I – um – This is the master bathroom. You will note it's unusually spacious for a bathroom. (He goes inside.) Do come in. I'd particularly like to draw your attention to this unusual mosaic round the shower depicting a traditional Maori rain ritual.
	(They have all followed him into the bathroom now and the door closes. There is a long, agonising pause, the handle turns and then a loud banging and shouting breaks out – they are all locked in. MISS JOHNSON hurries out of the kitchen and looks up. She hustles up the stairs and tries to force the door.)
MISS JOHNSON	(normal voice) I can't do it, I can't do it, Mr. – Mis-ter Pitt I cannot ze door open.
PITT	(calls) Then get someone to – then get something to help you.
MISS JOHNSON	Just a minute, please. (She calls over the balustrade.) Yvonne! Yvonne!
YVONNE	(rushing in) What is it now? I was just going.
MISS JOHNSON	You can't leave yet. They're all locked in the bathroom.
YVONNE	But he'll be doing his nut down the drive.
MISS JOHNSON	You'll have to show me how to get that door open.
YVONNE	(rushing up the stairs) What an afternoon. I have got one of me queer turns coming on now.
	(She arrives at the bathroom door and together they force it open. As the door swings back, MISS JOHNSON steps back to the right and YVONNE to the left. PITT is the first out.)

PITT	(as he comes out) Terribly sorry about that, Sir Lindsay. Most emba-a-a- (He sees YVONNE and repeats the previous routine with gestures and exercises.)	

(YVONNE dives for the nearest cover, which happens to be the master bedroom.)

- most embarrassing.

SIR LINDSAY   (giving him a strange look) These things will happen in the best regulated homes.

(MISS JOHNSON goes out to the kitchen.)

MELANIE   (coming out with LADY COOPER) Thank you, Olga.

PITT   Helga! You can go back now, Helga!

MELANIE   Yes, Helga, have you got rid of that little bundle of rubbish?

PITT   She hasn't been able to, darling, because some of it's in the bed - some of it's up - (He surreptitiously indicates the bedroom.) Perhaps you'd like to see the main guest room, Lady Cooper? (He opens the door for her.)

LADY COOPER   (as she goes in) Does this have a circular bed as well, Mr. Pitt?

PITT   No, this room's quite normal. (To MELANIE.) Come along, darling. After you, Sir Lindsay.

SIR LINDSAY   Thank you very much. (Going into room behind the others.) This is a very good size as well.

(As SIR LINDSAY goes in, YVONNE comes out of the master bedroom and makes for the stairs. While she is doing so, SIR LINDSAY starts coming out of the room again. She does the only thing possible and dives into the bathroom. PITT, who is still in the doorway, just catches sight of her going in.)

(To PITT, in doorway.) Very satisfactory.

	I say, old chap, do you mind if I just pop into your bathroom?
PITT	(aghast) Is it really essential? I mean, can't you – couldn't you hold?
SIR LINDSAY	(already there and trying the door) I say, it's locked.
PITT	(aside) Thank heaven!
SIR LINDSAY	(confidentially) Funny girl, your Miss Johansenn. She's in there again.
PITT	Yes, we're thinking of sending her to see Dr. Rothenstein. There's another bathroom downstairs if you can hold on a minute.
SIR LINDSAY	Needs must, I suppose.
PITT	(going to bedroom R. as MELANIE and LADY COOPER emerge from first guest room) This is the second guest room, Sir Lindsay.
SIR LINDSAY	(following him with the obvious business) Very convenient, yes.
LADY COOPER	I wonder if I could just use your bathroom to powder my nose, Mrs. Pitt?
MELANIE	Do, by all means.
PITT	No, no!
SIR LINDSAY	(turning) You can't at the moment, my dear. Miss Johansenn's in there again.
	(At this moment MISS JOHNSON runs in breathless from the kitchen. Not realising that they are talking about her, she picks artificial flowers from window box and goes out to kitchen with them and returns.)
LADY COOPER	But Miss Johansenn's down there.
PITT	(desperately) It's that lock – it's stuck again. I'll have to force it later – when you've gone.
SIR LINDSAY	No time like the present. Let me give you a hand, old chap. (Crossing to bathroom

Scene 1   UPROAR IN THE HOUSE   35

	and starting to force door.) We'll soon have this open.
PITT	(aghast) No, no, no. Yvonne's - if you heave on that you might do yourself an injury. And then you'd have to go back to Doctor Rothenstein. That would never do, would it?
SIR LINDSAY	(stopping his effort) You're right! It would not.
LADY COOPER	Is there another bathroom in the house, Mrs. Pitt?
MELANIE	Another bathroom? Well - er - oh - that is -
PITT	Yes, yes, there's another bathroom in the au pair's suite and I want you all to see it - straight away.
	(PITT ushers them down the stairs: first LADY COOPER, then MELANIE, SIR LINDSAY and finally PITT himself. MISS JOHNSON is standing at the bottom of the stairs. As PITT starts to descend, a plaintive voice calls from the bathroom.)
YVONNE	Help! Please help me!
PITT	(hissing towards her) You'll have to wait till I get back.
SIR LINDSAY	What did you say, old chap?
PITT	(between clenched teeth) I said you'll have to wait until you see the back of the house - (Smiling broadly.) - it's even nicer than the front.
SIR LINDSAY	Oh, is it - is it really?
LADY COOPER	(now at bottom of stairs) Where is the au pair's suite, Mrs. Pitt?
MELANIE	The au pair's suite? Well, that - that's over there. (She does not know, so she gives a general expansive gesture.)

(LADY COOPER starts U.L. MISS JOHNSON gestures U.R. to MELANIE, who grabs LADY COOPER by the arm.)

No, you misunderstood me – I meant over there.

(MELANIE conducts LADY COOPER U.R., followed by SIR LINDSAY and PITT.)

PITT (as he passes MISS JOHNSON, hissing) Get hold of that clottish girl!

SIR LINDSAY Beg your pardon?

PITT I said we nearly sold to a Scottish earl, you know.

SIR LINDSAY Did you?

PITT Yes, but then he decided it wasn't sufficiently remote.

SIR LINDSAY Extraordinary. Seemed remote enough to me when we ended up in that chicken farm.
(He trips over the step U.R. and disappears, with the others, into the au pair's suite.)

(MISS JOHNSON runs upstairs and with a lot of difficulty forces open the bathroom door.)

MISS JOHNSON Quick, before they come out again.

YVONNE (clattering down the stairs) Oh, what a rave up. I never thought selling houses would turn out like this. Hiding in bathrooms – it's enough to send you psyche-delicate.

MISS JOHNSON Just get in Lockwood's car and go. I'm going to fix that lock once and for all.

YVONNE (now opening the kitchen door) Blimey, it's them. (She runs D.L., opens the front door and goes out.)

(At the same time, MISS JOHNSON starts up the stairs as MELANIE and LADY COOPER come in through the kitchen door U.L.)

LADY COOPER (as she comes in) How very convenient having the au pair's suite communicating with the kitchen.

Scene 1   UPROAR IN THE HOUSE

MELANIE	(as if realising it for the first time) I suppose it is, really.
LADY COOPER	(seeing MISS JOHNSON disappearing into the bathroom) Good gracious, that girl's going in there again: what is she up to?
MELANIE	About chapter fifteen I should think.
LADY COOPER	Where does that door lead to over there? (She points D.R.)
MELANIE	(again she does not know) That door over there? That door over there is the – er – is the – er –
MISS JOHNSON	(coming out of bathroom and overhearing) Nursery. (She disappears into the master bedroom.)
LADY COOPER	Ah, the nursery.
MELANIE	Yes, I said the nursery. Would you like to see it?
LADY COOPER	There's no need to bother. I can't get over that tree. Most unusual. What sort is it?
MELANIE	Oh, it's a spruce – a tropical spruce, of course. It has to be because of the central heating.
LADY COOPER	Of course. (The conversation is now beginning to run out. She is strangely disinterested and has been throughout. There is an awkward pause. For want of something better to do, she picks up the children's photograph.) All these children yours?
MELANIE	Yes, all four are ours.
LADY COOPER	But there are only three here.
MELANIE	Are there? Oh, I was forgetting little Jamie wasn't born then. That was taken three years ago.
LADY COOPER	Really? Judging by this photograph, your eldest boy must be – what – eleven now?
MELANIE	Yes, he is. Maximilian's twelve next birthday.

LADY COOPER	You look so young to have a boy that age. You must've married very early.
MELANIE	Yes, we did. Actually, we ran away to Gretna Green together.
LADY COOPER	(putting down photograph) How very romantic. (She crosses and sits on tree seat.) They're all striking children, Mrs. Pitt, particularly the girl. What's her name?
MELANIE	(coming D.C.) Her name? Oh - er - Lesley. Lesley Anne. Yes, we're all one big happy family here, the five of us - the six of us.
	(MISS JOHNSON comes out of the master bedroom with a screwdriver and re-enters the bathroom.)
LADY COOPER	By the way, what does your husband do for a living?
MELANIE	He's a sales executive.
LADY COOPER	And what exactly does he sell?
MELANIE	He sells house - (Suddenly realising what she is saying.) - how super, here they are now. (She breaks behind tree seat to right of tree.)
	(PITT and SIR LINDSAY enter U.L.)
PITT	(coming in) As you can see, Sir Lindsay, the architect has combined the subtle use of space and levels to capture the ever-changing moods of modern living.
SIR LINDSAY	(falling down the step U.L.) There are a lot of stairs, aren't there? Ah, here are the ladies. I wonder what they've been saying behind our back, eh, old chap?
PITT	(apprehensively) So do I.
SIR LINDSAY	(to C.) I can't get over that tree. Never seen one in a house before. Exactly what sort is it?
PITT	It's a larch -

	UPROAR IN THE HOUSE	
LADY COOPER	But your wife just told me it was a spruce - a tropical spruce.	
PITT	Yes, I was just going to say it's a spruce - a very larch tropical spruce.	
SIR LINDSAY	It's one of the things that worries me about this house. We might have to have it felled. We've got a couple of dogs, you know - labradors, too. Have you got any pets?	
PITT	No pets, Sir Lindsay, just our children.	
SIR LINDSAY	Yes, I don't suppose children - ? No - Still, nothing like children around the place to make a happy home. How many have you got, old chap?	
PITT	(starting counting, looking at MELANIE) Well, let's see now, there's one - two - three - (Getting alarmed.) - four -

(MELANIE gives him the signal.)

- four - FOUR, that's it. We've got four. | |
SIR LINDSAY	Boys or girls?	
PITT	Yes.	
SIR LINDSAY	Well, which?	
PITT	Er - ah - (He looks at MELANIE for signal guidance.) Well, there's one boy - no, one girl and three boys. Yes, that's right, one girl and three boys.	
LADY COOPER	I was just saying to your wife what a striking child Lesley is.	
PITT	Yes, he's a strapping little lad. Very good at rugger for his age, Sir Lindsay.	
MELANIE	(coming between SIR LINDSAY and PITT) No, darling, Lady Cooper was talking about Lesley Anne, our nine year old daughter, not our second son, Leslie-Leslie.	
PITT	It's a bit confusing having two Lesleys. It's an old family name, you know - on Great Aunt Lesley's side.	
MELANIE	(pointedly) At least we never confuse our

Scene 1 — 39

	eldest and youngest, Jamie and Maximilian, do we, darling?
PITT	No. Of course, he's a big chap now, Jamie –
	(MELANIE breaks behind PITT to right of contemporary chair.)
	– nearly as tall as I am.
LADY COOPER	But your wife said he's only three.
PITT	Yes, and he's nearly as tall as I am when I'm sitting down – on the floor, of course.
SIR LINDSAY	(sitting down in the modern chair C. and practically disappearing from view in it) I'm sorry we shan't be meeting your delightful family, Mr. Pitt, particularly as I understand you're moving in the very near future.
PITT	Yes, we hope to be moving out very soon. That's the reason why we're anxious to sell as quickly as possible. As you know, we want to sell with furniture and fittings and I was wondering how you feel about it, now you've had a good look round?
SIR LINDSAY	I'm going to be perfectly frank, old chap. I'm an individualist.
PITT	(fearing the worst) Oh.
SIR LINDSAY	(struggling out of the chair and breaking L.) I'm not keen on ultra modern houses and this really is ultra modern. So often these places are just a house and not a home, don't you think?
PITT	But not in this case. As you've probably gathered, if ever there was a happy home – (He crosses to MELANIE and puts his arm round her shoulder.) – excuse me – this is it.
MELANIE	(putting both arms round him and drawing him close) Thank you, darling. That's the nicest thing you've ever said to me.
PITT	(trying to disentangle himself) And I meant every word of it – darling.

Scene 1	UPROAR IN THE HOUSE	41

SIR LINDSAY I'm sure you did. I'm very sensitive to atmosphere, and there's been a very definite atmosphere here this afternoon.

PITT You noticed?

SIR LINDSAY I noticed everything.   (Agonising pause.) That's why I've definitely decided I do not want to waste my time – beating about the bush. It's a happy family home and I want to buy it.

PITT You do?

SIR LINDSAY I do: subject to contract, naturally. I understand the original builders are acting as the agents for you.

PITT Lockwood's Luxury Homesteads, that's right.

SIR LINDSAY Good. I'll pop in and see their Sales Manager first thing tomorrow.

PITT (crossing below armchair to SIR LINDSAY, aghast)   No, no, no, I won't be there – I mean I happen to know he won't be there. Mr. Lockwood is handling this personally: he's responsible for the whole thing. He's a very good friend of mine.

SIR LINDSAY Is he? He's a friend of mine, too. Small world, isn't it?

PITT Isn't it?

SIR LINDSAY Charming chap, as well.

PITT Charming.

SIR LINDSAY (a straight gesture with the hand) Straight as they come.

PITT (a wavy gesture)   Straight as they come.

SIR LINDSAY Well, we'd better be off now. We've got a hotel room booked at Edenfield. How far is it from here?

PITT About forty miles.

SIR LINDSAY As far as that, is it? We'd better get cracking then. Come along, my dear.

LADY COOPER	Goodbye, Mrs. Pitt. So nice to have met you. (She goes up to T.V. for gloves, etc. and moves down to main entrance.)
MELANIE	And you, Lady Cooper.
SIR LINDSAY	(pressing a pound note into MELANIE's hand) See you again, I hope. (Quietly.) Buy a little something for the children from me, my dear.
PITT	No, no, Sir Lindsay, we couldn't, we really couldn't.
SIR LINDSAY	Of course you can, whenever they come back from – wherever they are.
PITT) MELANIE)	(together) Granny's – Auntie's –
SIR LINDSAY	When they come. (MISS JOHNSON appears out of the bathroom.) Goodbye, Miss Johansenn. (Precisely.) I do hope you are feeling better now.
MISS JOHNSON	Oh – ja – oui, oui –
SIR LINDSAY	That's the idea. (He trips over the step and goes out D.L. with LADY COOPER. PITT collapses in the chair C.)
PITT	Now, Miss Johnson, you'd better start packing up. (MISS JOHNSON goes out to the Nursery.)
MELANIE	Don't sit down, darling. (She hands him the pound note.) You'd better pop out and buy some sweets for our three year old giant.
PITT	Don't speak to me. It was a nightmare. I thought this was going to be the proudest day of my life: instead, I've been degraded and humiliated by that dreadful man Lockwood. And what's going to happen when the Coopers move in and find their

	Conservative candidate's taken part in a gigantic confidence trick?
MELANIE	Isn't that what they do every election, darling? (She sits R. end of tree seat.)
PITT	No, they do not. (He rises and crosses to her.) And don't keep calling me 'darling'! If I'd known it was going to turn out like this I'd never have done it. I wasn't given time to think. My political career's ruined: twelve hard years in the Young Conservatives for nothing.
MELANIE	It's a pity, really. You'd have made a lovely M.P. - you lie so beautifully, darling.
PITT	There you go again. Don't keep calling me 'darling'! This sort of thing's easy for you - you're a professional actress.
MISS JOHNSON	(coming in D.R. with the coats) And what about me? How would you like to go into the bathroom as an English secretary and come out as a Swedish au pair? (She puts MELANIE's coat L. end of tree seat and hands PITT's coat to him.)
PITT	That's the least of my worries.
MISS JOHNSON	I don't see what you're worried about. Now we've sold the house, Mr. Lockwood will do anything to cover up for you.
PITT	Of course, I've sold it, haven't I? I was forgetting that - I think it was jolly clever how I pulled it off.
MELANIE	How you pulled it off?
PITT	Yes. Hurry up, Miss Johnson. I'm sure Miss Sinclair won't mind giving you a hand.
	(During the ensuing dialogue, MISS JOHNSON proceeds to collect various items of dressing and place them on the love seat in the centre of the room. MELANIE moves up to PITT, who helps her on with her coat.)

MELANIE	Sorry, Nigel, I'm afraid our forty minutes of married bliss must come to a sudden end. I'm meeting my fiance tonight, and he doesn't like to be kept waiting. I shan't be contesting our divorce and you can have the custody of the children. (She breaks D.L.)
PITT	Thank you very much.
	(The door to the kitchen U.L. bursts open and YVONNE staggers in, everything awry.)
YVONNE	He went without me! He went without me!
MISS JOHNSON	What have you been doing, Yvonne? Look at you.
YVONNE	The fog's so thick out there, I couldn't even see me own feet. I wish I'd never come.
PITT	You're not the only one, I can assure you.
MELANIE	I can give you a lift into town if that's any use.
YVONNE	We'll never make it. It's like a pea soup out there. My dad'll go bersuck, I know he will –
	(The door chimes sound and stick. PITT crosses and peeps out through the venetian blinds.)
PITT	Who's that? My God, they're back – Sir Lindsay and Lady Cooper. (He rushes down and kicks the door jamb. The chimes stop.)
MISS JOHNSON	Back? They can't be.
PITT	They are. They must've left something behind.
MELANIE	Perhaps they've changed their mind about the house.
PITT	They can't do that. They said we'd sold it to them.
	(The door chimes again. PITT rushes down and kicks it again. They stop.)
	Get the place straight again – get that

Scene 1   UPROAR IN THE HOUSE   45

	picture up. (To MELANIE.) Get your coat off. (To YVONNE.) And you - get out of here.
YVONNE	Where can I go to?
PITT	I don't care where you go - just go.
YVONNE	It's not right I should be shoved around like this. I'm only sixteen. I've only just reached the age of content - (She goes U.L.)
	(During this conversation, MISS JOHNSON has rushed back up the ladder with the painting, which she hangs upside down and crooked in her haste. MELANIE goes into the nursery with her coat. As she tries to come out she meets MISS JOHNSON trying to get in with the stepladder. There is a moment of confusion during which PITT goes quietly to pieces. The chimes ring again, and PITT has to do the kicking routine again. MELANIE shoots to the tree-seat and sits down with a magazine. MISS JOHNSON rushes towards the au pair's suite and leaves the door ajar so that she can peep out. PITT opens the door.)
SIR LINDSAY	Sorry to trouble you again, old chap.
PITT	(panting heavily) Not at all, Sir Lindsay. We were just settling down for a quiet evening together.
SIR LINDSAY	I don't suppose you've noticed but there's a terrible fog outside.
PITT	Is there?
LADY COOPER	Absolutely shocking, Mr. Pitt.
SIR LINDSAY	I was wondering if we could use your telephone for an urgent call.
PITT	Is that all - I mean, is that all we can do for you?
SIR LINDSAY	(shutting front door and crossing to phone) Well, no. Since you mention it, old chap, as

46 UPROAR IN THE HOUSE ACT I

> it's quite impossible to drive, we were wondering if you'd mind putting us up for the night?
>
> (There is a gasp from the au pair's suite and the door slams. PITT and MELANIE react in horror and despair.)
>
> And is the bathroom free now?
>
> CURTAIN

Scene 2

When the curtain rises, PITT and MELANIE are discovered alone on stage. An argument is in progress, although voices are lowered.

PITT But you can't possibly leave now. How am I going to explain it to the Coopers?

MELANIE I don't know. Tell them I've had to go to the youngest children.

PITT I can't do that. I've already told them they're staying at their grandmother's.

MELANIE So I've gone to their grandmother's.

PITT You'll have a job. I've already said their grandmother lives in Harrogate.

MELANIE What on earth did you say that for?

PITT I had to say something. Besides, my mother does live in Harrogate. Anyway, you were the one who produced four children this afternoon, not me.

MELANIE If you hadn't left me alone I'd never have had four children, would I?

PITT No, and you're not the first woman who's said that either. What a terrible scandal if this ever gets out. I'll never be able to speak in public again. (Realising.) Speak in – my God! I was supposed to be speaking to the Young Conservatives tonight at half past seven. (Looking at watch.)

	I might just make it. (He crosses to the front door.)
MELANIE	(following him) You can't possibly leave now. How am I going to explain it to the Coopers?
PITT	This is disastrous. I'll miss my first public engagement as candidate. That's all I need now. I'm finished if they find out I've spent the night with you instead of the Free Trade Area.
MELANIE	(loudly) Damn the Free Trade Area, damn the Conservative Party, and damn their newly adopted candidate as well.
PITT	(loudly) Don't shout like that. Can you imagine what Cooper would do to my reputation if he knew the truth?
	(The telephone tinkles.)
	He's on that bedroom phone again. (Crossing to C.) Who can he be ringing at this time of night?
MELANIE	(following him to C.) I don't care what's going on in <u>his</u> bedroom, I'm more concerned about what's supposed to be going on in ours.
PITT	OURS? What on earth are you talking about?
MELANIE	The master bedroom up there. The one where mummy and daddy are supposed to share that circular bed.
PITT	Circular bed? I can assure you that there will be no La Rendezvousing tonight. (He sits on tree seat.) I am a prospective parliamentary candidate, and –
MELANIE	Yes, I know all about that, but I suppose even politicians have to look on the practical side of things from time to time.
PITT	Yes, once every five years or when there's a General Election. What's that got to do with it?
MELANIE	Hasn't it occurred to you that our guests

	will expect us to share a room tonight? We are supposed to be husband and wife, and it is normal for a husband and wife to sleep together.
PITT	(rising) Sleep together? It's out of the question. What would my party agent say?
MELANIE	Why, you don't sleep with him, do you?
PITT	Certainly not. How dare you insinuate such a thing!
MELANIE	(crossing and sitting in contemporary armchair) More to the point, what would David Prosser say?
PITT	Prosser? Who's David Prosser?
MELANIE	My fiance David Prosser, M.A., Bachelor of Law. What will he say - I haven't been able to get in touch with him.
PITT	(going to R. of MELANIE) He won't say anything, because I shall be occupying the other guest room tonight.
MELANIE	I'm delighted to hear it. But won't it rather destroy the image of that happy family home Sir Lindsay's so keen on buying?
PITT	All right, they see us going into the same room together. That doesn't stop me coming out again afterwards when -
	(LADY COOPER comes out of the first guest room and starts down the stairs. PITT is "alerted" by MELANIE and immediately changes the subject.)
	- I'm sure Sir Lindsay and Lady Cooper will understand if dinner is a little frugal, dear. (Breaking round to above tree seat.) After all, we were expecting to be out tonight ourselves, weren't we?
MELANIE	Yes, we were.
PITT	(now deliberately noticing LADY COOPER and moving to her) Ah, Lady Cooper. I didn't see you coming. Everything all right?

LADY COOPER	Yes, thank you, Mr. Pitt. Sir Lindsay's just finishing a phone call.
PITT	Good, dinner won't be long. Melanie was just going to see how Helga's getting on with it – weren't you, dear?
LADY COOPER	What a pity. I hoped we were going to have another little talk about your charming children.
PITT	That's what I thought.
MELANIE	I'd love to, Lady Cooper. But I must keep an eye on things in the kitchen. (Going off and giving PITT an 'Over to you' look.) You will excuse me, won't you? (She goes out through kitchen door U.L.)
LADY COOPER	What a lovely girl your wife, is Mr. Pitt. (Crossing and sitting on tree seat.) If it isn't a rude question, how did you come to meet her?
PITT	Oh, we were thrown together as it were – quite unexpectedly. Do you know, I remember it as if it were only today.
LADY COOPER	Your wife looks so young. She must've married very early.
PITT	Yes, she did. (Floundering). Let's see, there's a gir .... a boy of twelve and I'm .... I'm .... yes .... and we were both the same age – twenty two.
LADY COOPER	But your wife was telling me earlier you had to run away together to get married. Why did you do that if you were twenty two?
PITT	No, you misunderstood me. Melanie and I were both the same age. She was twenty and I was twenty too – you know, as well. And we ran away together to Ireland.
LADY COOPER	To Ireland? I understood you went to Gretna Green.
PITT	(breaking L. and turning) Yes, we did. But we went to Ireland first to put her

	father off the scent. Then we went to Gretna Green via Holy - er - Liverpool - (Thankfully seeing SIR LINDSAY coming out of the first guest room.) Ah, here comes Sir Lindsay. I'm so glad - I mean I'm so glad because dinner must be nearly ready. (He crosses towards kitchen.) Did you get through all right, Sir Lindsay?
SIR LINDSAY	Yes, thank you, old chap. You must let me pay for the calls.
PITT	Certainly not. I wouldn't dream of it. Well, I must go and wash - dish - er carve up in the kitchen.
	(PITT is about to go out in some confusion when LADY COOPER notices the pyjamas and nightdress inside the tree seat. She picks them up and turns to PITT.)
LADY COOPER	Excuse me, are these meant to be here?
PITT	(aghast) Good gracious no. (He crosses hurriedly.) It's that au pair of ours; I've never come across such an untidy girl. She's always putting things round the tree - seems to think it's Christmas all the time - what one might call Santa Claustrophobia, I suppose - (He breaks into nervous laughter and goes out U.L. in a welter of embarrassment and night clothes.)
	(There is a pause. SIR LINDSAY and LADY COOPER look at each other.)
LADY COOPER	(rising and crossing below SIR LINDSAY to make sure the kitchen door is closed) I'm sorry, Sir Lindsay, I don't think I can go through with this. I'm absolutely certain they suspect what I am.
SIR LINDSAY	Nonsense, my dear Mrs. - oh dear, I keep on forgetting your name.
LADY COOPER	Hamilton - Dulcie Hamilton, and I'm sure they know I'm not the real Lady Cooper. You realise that if there's any smell of collusion, I shall never work again. (She

	sits in contemporary chair.) There won't be a decent divorce solicitor in the country who'll touch me with a bargepole.
SIR LINDSAY	You do yourself an injustice, my dear. If the present Lady Cooper was as charming as you, I wouldn't be trying to give her grounds for divorce and you wouldn't be here.
LADY COOPER	I suppose you say that to all your professional co-respondents?
SIR LINDSAY	(with a chuckle) Now, now, Mrs. Hamilton, this is the first time and - all being well tonight - the last.
LADY COOPER	Did you get through to Mr. Carless all right?
SIR LINDSAY	Mr. Carless? Yes, I caught him just before he set out for the hotel. He knows where we are now and I've told him to get here with his camera tonight, if he has to crawl on his hands and knees.
LADY COOPER	I know you're a busy man, Sir Lindsay, but we could have made it another night - at a compromise fee, of course.
SIR LINDSAY	That's very accommodating of you, but as soon as I've got this house tied up for the future Lady Cooper, I'm off to the Bahamas while this blows over. That's why I want the evidence for my divorce supplied now in black and white.
LADY COOPER	I'm sure Mr. Carless is very experienced in hotel assignments, but this is a little different. He won't know which room we're in.
SIR LINDSAY	You obviously know your job, my dear. It was the first question he asked. Have you worked with him before?
LADY COOPER	No, this is the first time I've been on his circuit. What sort of man is he?
SIR LINDSAY	I've no idea. I've never met him personally. My solicitor made all the arrangements, of course.

LADY COOPER	But how is he going to know which room we're in?
SIR LINDSAY	No need to worry about that: it's all arranged. He's going to call here on some pretext or other and I shall tip him off – on the quiet, of course. Just one thing. What exactly am I supposed to do tonight?
LADY COOPER	Nothing.
SIR LINDSAY	Oh. Nothing at all?
LADY COOPER	You'd better sit on my bed while he takes the photograph, but that's all. It's lucky the room's got twin beds in it. We shall both be able to get a good night's sleep.
SIR LINDSAY	Yes. Rather a shame we had to involve the Pitts in this – such a genuine couple. Unusual these days to find people who don't put on an act when entertaining.
	(PITT comes in from kitchen U.L.)
PITT	(coming down L. of LADY COOPER) Dinner's almost ready. I'm afraid it's a bit of a scratch meal, but you know how these things are?
SIR LINDSAY	Indeed I do. As I've just been saying to Lady Hamilton – Lady Cooper, I'm afraid we've caught you out.
PITT	(faltering) Caught us out?
SIR LINDSAY	You know, caught you with your trousers down –
	(PITT reacts.)
	– without food in the larder when the family's away. You didn't bargain for us or the fog, did you?
PITT	No, we certainly didn't. Still, let's make the best of what we've got. After you, Lady Cooper. (He ushers them towards the dining area U.C.)
	(LADY COOPER goes in and SIR LINDSAY

SIR LINDSAY	stands back for PITT.) Carry on, old chap. (PITT goes in and SIR LINDSAY is about to follow when the door chimes sound and stick.) Don't worry – I'll get it. (He deliberately closes the sliding door to the dining room, leaving PITT inside. SIR LINDSAY blandly kicks the jamb. The chimes stop. Through the front door steps DAVID PROSSER. He is about 40, tall and bespectacled. He is the sort of man in whom MELANIE has seen security – albeit pretty dull security. PROSSER's world is bounded on the one hand by his law books and a fund of Latin tags, and on the other by his mother. His knowledge of the law is not equalled by his knowledge of life, and in PITT's hands he is shortly to prove nothing but unwilling clay. PROSSER crosses to SIR LINDSAY.) (Hissing.) Carless?
PROSSER	I beg your pardon?
SIR LINDSAY	Douglas Carless?
PROSSER	(proffering his hand) How do you do, Mr. Carless?
SIR LINDSAY	No, I'm not Carless – I thought you were.
PROSSER	Who?
SIR LINDSAY	Carless.
PROSSER	No, I'm not Carless, I'm Prosser – David Prosser.
PITT	(coming into the room and almost jumping in the air in alarm) Prosser! (He rushes down to the door and grasps PROSSER's hand before another word can be spoken.) Prosser – Hello, Prosser, old man. How very nice to see you again.

(PROSSER looks at PITT blankly.)

However did you get here?

PROSSER (completely nonplussed) I came in my car and it was terrible. It took me two hours to cover fifteen miles. Mother will be most worried about me.

PITT I'm sure she will. To tell you the truth, David, you're the last person we expected to see tonight. Do join Lady Cooper in the dining room, Sir Lindsay. I shan't be a minute.

SIR LINDSAY Very well. Sorry about that little misunderstanding, Prosser, old chap. I quite thought you were someone else. (He goes into the dining area.)

PROSSER (crossing to C.) Excuse me, who exactly was that?

PITT (joining PROSSER) That's Sir Lindsay Cooper. He's staying here with Lady Cooper.

PROSSER I see. And if you don't mind me asking, who exactly are you?

PITT I'm Nigel Pitt.

PROSSER Nigel Pitt. I see. I'm David Prosser, you know.

PITT Yes, I know.

PROSSER But we've never met before, have we?

PITT No, of course we haven't.

PROSSER Then why did you imply you knew me when I came in?

PITT Because I didn't want Sir Lindsay to know I didn't know you, and you didn't know me.

PROSSER But I don't know you and you don't know me – do we?

PITT No, but he doesn't know that we don't know each other and it's most important that he doesn't.

Scene 2 UPROAR IN THE HOUSE 55

PROSSER	Why? I don't know him, do I?
PITT	No, of course you don't but he knows your fiancee.
PROSSER	Does he know Melanie? I didn't know she knew him. I've come here to fetch her.
PITT	Fetch her? You can't possibly fetch her tonight.
PROSSER	Why not? She's still here, isn't she? I saw her car outside.
PITT	Yes, of course she's still here, but she can't leave now.
PROSSER	She must leave now. We're supposed to be taking Mother out to celebrate our engagement tonight. She's been waiting with her fur on since half-past five. That's why I've struggled all this way to fetch Melanie.
PITT	(bringing him downstage) I'm sorry you've come all this way for nothing.
PROSSER	Nothing?
PITT	Yes, I'm afraid it's vital that she spends the evening with me.
PROSSER	With you? But I don't even know you. Who are you, anyway?
PITT	Don't let's start all that again. It's not who I am, it's what everyone thinks we are - Melanie and I.
PROSSER	Melanie and you? But who do they think you are?
PITT	Ah, that's it, you see. (He leads PROSSER to the tree seat.) Now, Prosser, old man, I want you to keep perfectly calm -
PROSSER	(sitting) Calm, yes.
PITT	Because I realise this may come as a bit of a shock.
PROSSER	Bit of a shock, yes.

PITT		But owing to an unfortunate combination of circumstances completely beyond our control –
PROSSER		Control, yes.
PITT		Sir Lindsay and Lady Cooper, our unexpected and highly respectable guests –
PROSSER		Respectable, yes.
PITT		They are under the impression – the mistaken impression, of course, that your fiancee and I are – er – married with four children.
PROSSER		Married, yes. (He reacts violently.) MARRIED WITH –
		(PITT claps a hand over his mouth and practically flattens him on the tree seat.)
PITT		Don't raise your voice like that. You'll ruin everything – yourself included. (He removes his hand.)
PROSSER		Myself? I'm not involved in this.
PITT		(clapping his hand on again) Oh yes, you are. Just by coming here you are. You're involved in this as much as we are. (He frog marches PROSSER towards the kitchen.) You'd better come into the kitchen and see Melanie. She'll explain.
PROSSER		(as they go) I'm not getting involved in anything. I'm a practising solicitor – and a – Rotarian. Oh, corruptis optimi pessima.
PITT		What did you say?
PROSSER		Optimi pessima.
PITT		Just as well I understood that –
		(The kitchen door closes. SIR LINDSAY comes out of the dining area.)
SIR LINDSAY		(in the doorway) I don't know what's happened to them. (He calls) Pitt – are you there, Pitt? (He crosses to the kitchen door and opens it.)

	(Through the open doorway comes PITT's voice.)
PITT	It it goes wrong now everything will blow up in our face – Oh, Sir Lindsay. (He comes out hurriedly, closing the door behind him.)
SIR LINDSAY	Everything all right, old chap? You seem to be in some sort of trouble.
PITT	(walking him towards the loveseat) Trouble? Good gracious, no. Whatever gave you that idea? Just a spot of bother with the – the gas stove. There seems to be an air lock. I was saying that if it goes wrong now everything – everything could blow up in our face. (He pulls SIR LINDSAY away just as he is about to sit down.) Do – do – do – do come back into the dining room; everything's ready. (He opens kitchen door and calls inside.) Miss John – Miss Johansenn, we're waiting for dinner.
	(As he and SIR LINDSAY go back in the dining area.)
	So sorry you've been kept waiting. She's got terribly lethargic that girl. (Going into the dining area.) Misses the sauna baths, I think.
	(The kitchen door opens and MISS JOHNSON hurries out carrying a soup tureen. She goes into the dining area and starts to serve the soup to SIR LINDSAY, LADY COOPER and PITT, who has had to make a show of sitting down. As MISS JOHNSON comes out of the kitchen, MELANIE's voice is heard briefly.)
MELANIE	But I can't let him down now –
MISS JOHNSON	(as she goes in with the soup) Ze hot soup, sir. Svedish chicken noodle.
	(The kitchen door opens and PROSSER emerges pulling MELANIE by the arm. Unseen by the others, he takes her towards the front door.)

PROSSER	I don't care if he is a Conservative candidate, Melanie. I can't allow you to stay in this house a minute longer.	
MELANIE	David, you're hurting my arm. I've never seen you like this before.	
PROSSER	And I've never seen you like this before. I won't let you be a party to it. Mother would never get over it. (He opens the front door.)	
MELANIE	But I can't go like this without seeing – NI – GEL! (Her voice rises as she almost trips over the step and the door closes behind her and PROSSER.)	

(PITT, hearing her voice, jumps up from the dinner table and rushes out.)

PITT   Excuse me, I think I heard my wife calling. (He comes into the empty room, looks round and hurries to the kitchen, calling.) Melanie – where are you, Melanie? (He looks into the kitchen, reacts, then hastens across to the nursery door D.R. and looks inside.) Melanie – is that you, Melanie?

(YVONNE emerges, eyes blinking.)

YVONNE   No, it's not – it's me.

PITT   Oh, my God, I'd forgotten you were still here.

YVONNE   (tearfully) So's everybody else by the look of it. I've been in here for hours. When am I going to get some nosh?

PITT   In a minute – in a minute. We're in real trouble now. What's happened to my – to Melanie, Miss Sinclair?

YVONNE   She's gone.

PITT   GONE?

YVONNE   Yeah. That other bloke carted her off. I was looking out for the nosh and I saw them going through the front door.

PITT	(now beside himself) What? She can't leave me in the lurch like this. It's an impossible situation. The whole thing will come out in the open now and the sale will fall through, I know it will. What can I possibly say if Sir Lindsay asks me where my wife is - ?
	(SIR LINDSAY emerges from the dining area. YVONNE dives back in the nursery.)
SIR LINDSAY	I say, old chap, where's your wife? Her soup's getting cold.
	(During this conversation, MISS JOHNSON goes back into the kitchen with the soup tureen.)
PITT	My wife? Oh, my wife. She's - she's just gone down the bottom of the garden to get some parsley. I'd better see if I can find her. (He starts for the door.) I shan't be a minute, you go and finish your soup.
SIR LINDSAY	I have finished it.
PITT	Oh. Miss Johansenn!
	(MISS JOHNSON appears in the kitchen doorway looking very harassed.)
	Bring on the next course at once! Our guests are waiting.
MISS JOHNSON	(in English) I'm doing my best - (She suddenly remembers.) - Meester Pitt.
	(The front door opens and MELANIE comes in followed by a remonstrating PROSSER.)
MELANIE	I'm sorry, David, but I'm not walking out like this. (She sees SIR LINDSAY.) Oh, Sir Lindsay, I thought you were having dinner.
SIR LINDSAY	So did I. You mustn't bother about the parsley on a night like this: it's far too cold.

MELANIE		Parsley?
		(Parsley business. PITT bends down and mimes the plucking of parsley behind SIR LINDSAY's back. SIR LINDSAY turns and reacts. PITT pretends he is dusting something off the floor. SIR LINDSAY points to something unseen, then brings down his foot heavily as if stamping on an insect. SIR LINDSAY picks up the invisible and offending microbe and tosses it into the tree seat. PITT looks on amazed. SIR LINDSAY turns to PROSSER.)
SIR LINDSAY		Ah, we meet again, Prosser, old chap. Have you got whatever it was you came for?
PROSSER		No, I haven't and I think, Sir Lindsay, it's about time that you were given a full and frank explanation –
PITT		(cutting in) I agree, I agree – a full and frank explanation of who Mr. Prosser is and why he is here.
PROSSER		But I am in no way responsible –
PITT		You're far too modest, Prosser, old man. You shouldn't hide your light under a bushel. You're very responsible – you have a very responsible position. He's with the Law you know, Sir Lindsay –
SIR LINDSAY		(alarmed) With the law? Is he? Oh dear – I mean, how interesting –
PITT		Yes, he's a solicitor.
SIR LINDSAY		A solicitor?
PITT		And he's doing very well. He should go a long way if he doesn't do or say anything that would prejudice his career. And I'm sure he won't because we know how sticky the Law Society can be over professional misconduct, don't we, Prosser old man?
SIR LINDSAY		(visibly shaken) Misconduct! What do you mean, misconduct?

PITT	Because a solicitor's behaviour must be beyond reproach, Sir Lindsay. He can't afford to be associated with anything dubious, can he, Prosser, old man?	
PROSSER	No, he can't. (He gulps.) Summum jus, summa injuria.	
PITT	Some are indeed!	
SIR LINDSAY	If Mr. Prosser's your solicitor then presumably he's going to deal with the conveyancing of this property?	
PROSSER	Certainly not - I'm having nothing to do with anything.	
PITT	No, he's not having anything to do with nothing because he specialises in arbitration cases: travels all over the country, don't you, Prosser?	
PROSSER	(beginning to fall into line) Y-y-yes.	
PITT	Which is why he's away so often and we were so surprised to see him tonight, wasn't it, darling?	
MELANIE	Yes, it was, darling.	
	(PROSSER winces.)	
SIR LINDSAY	It beats me how you managed to get here at all in this fog, old chap.	
PROSSER	Yes, it was difficult. But I was very worried about my marriage to - (He realises what he is saying and then makes it worse.) - about Miss - about Mel -	
PITT	(cutting in) About Hel-ga - he was worried about Helga.	
SIR LINDSAY	Helga? Miss Johansenn ?	
	(MISS JOHNSON comes out of the kitchen carrying a dish of potatoes baked in their jackets.)	
PITT	(not noticing her) Yes, you see he's married to her: she's not really Miss Johansenn at all - she's Mrs. Prosser.	

(This is too much for MISS JOHNSON. She drops the metal dish of potatoes with a gasp. MELANIE goes over to help her pick up the potatoes and obviously has a word in her ear. The potatoes are hot and difficult to pick up. The noise brings LADY COOPER out of the dining area.)

LADY COOPER
Am I missing something interesting?

SIR LINDSAY
I should just say you are, my dear. This gentleman here, Mr. Prosser, is actually a solicitor -

LADY COOPER
Oh, my God - oh, my god-father was a solicitor.

SIR LINDSAY
And that's not all: he's married to our Miss Johansenn here. She's not Miss Johansenn at all - she's Mrs. Prosser. How did you come to meet her, old chap?

PROSSER
(lost)   Well - er - I - that is -   (He calls pathetically.)   Mother!

PITT
(saving him)   He met her here actually, at Christmas. Swept her off her feet, didn't you, Prosser, old man?

PROSSER
Oooooo!

PITT
Oooooo! It was a lovely wedding. Her parents came over from Sweden and Mother came over from - Tunbridge Wells and then, almost immediately, he had to go and arbitrate all over the place. So Miss John - Miss Johan - Mrs. Prosser stayed on with us for a bit.

SIR LINDSAY
Somewhat unusual to have a married au pair, isn't it?

PITT
Yes, isn't it? Of course, David and Helga won't be staying with us much longer now they're expecting a happy event - a little Prosser.

PROSSER
(aghast)   A little Prosser!

(This is again too much for MISS JOHNSON who drops the dish and potatoes once again.)

SIR LINDSAY		My dear young lady, I had no idea you were in the family - you mustn't exert yourself on our account
PITT		No, of course not, Helga. It must have been a great shock to find you'd suddenly got a husband - home by your side, as it were, and not away - arbitrating -
PROSSER		Oh dear, I do think this is all very ill-advised. Things have gone a bit too far. I really think I ought to say -
PITT		Yes, I expect you've got a lot you want to say to your wife, David. Don't you worry about the dinner, Helga. You've got quite enough in the oven already. (He crosses MISS JOHNSON over next to PROSSER.) You two trot along to your flat and make yourself cosy - come along Lady Cooper, Sir Lindsay. We'll never finish dinner at this rate.
SIR LINDSAY		(going into dining area and handing potato dish to PITT) I must confess I'm still feeling a bit peckish. Very good food in this house but rather a long time between courses! (He disappears, laughing.)
PROSSER		(to PITT) I must insist upon having words with you in private, Mr. Pitt.
PITT		(hissing, handing potato dish to PROSSER) Not now - not now. I'll be with you in a minute. (He goes into dining area.)
MELANIE		Do go into the au pair's suite, David, there's a good boy. We're all in this together now.
PROSSER		But you don't seem to realise what you're asking me to do - to go off alone with a strange foreign lady.
MISS JOHNSON		I'm not foreign: I'm as English as you are.
PROSSER		(letting one end of the tray go so that the potatoes cascade to the floor) Good gracious. Whatever next?

MELANIE	(picking up potatoes) I'll tell you what's next – dinner, to keep them occupied while we get this sorted out. Give me those potatoes for a start.
YVONNE	(sticking her head out of the nursery door) Potatoes? (She rushes across the stage, grabs a couple of potatoes and rushes back to the nursery.) I must have something to eat – I'm absolutely ravished. (She disappears again.)
PROSSER	(astounded) Who was that?
MELANIE	(going towards kitchen) Oh, she's stopping here as well but we don't talk about her. (She goes into kitchen.)
PROSSER	I don't think I can stand much more of this – this is a madhouse. Young ladies hidden in rooms with hot potatoes –
MISS JOHNSON	I don't like this any more than you, but we've got to get it sorted out. (She takes him carefully by two fingers only.) Come along, Mr. Prosser, this way. (She leads him U.R.)
PROSSER	(shaking himself free) If this ever comes to light I shall be struck off. They're committing every offence you can think of. I've counted twelve in as many minutes – conspiring with intent to defraud or deceive – false pretence – misrepresentation – collusion – condoning a felony – aiding and abetting –
MISS JOHNSON	(hurrying back and dragging him off) Mr. Prosser!
	(They are gone. MELANIE hurries from the kitchen towards the dining area carrying two plates of food. As she is about to go inside, the door chimes ring out again and stick.)
MELANIE	The door!
SIR LINDSAY	(from dining room) Somebody else lost in the fog, eh?

Scene 2   UPROAR IN THE HOUSE   65

PITT	(appearing in the dining room doorway) The door!
MELANIE	(kicking the jamb and stopping the bell) I know. Take these plates: I'll see who it is.
	(MELANIE hands the very hot plates to PITT, who reacts accordingly. She is wearing oven gloves. He thrusts the plates back at her.)
PITT	(in agony and through clenched teeth) Never do that again. If you hadn't said 'Yes' when I was trying to say 'No', (He indicates the dining area.) - they wouldn't be here tonight.
MELANIE	I like that.
PITT	You leave it to me this time. Nobody else sets foot in this house tonight. (He crosses to the front door.)
	(MELANIE goes into dining area. PITT opens the door. Outside stand ANDREW and AUDREY GREY. He is forty, self-confident and forceful. She is about five years younger, intelligent and sophisticated.)
PITT	I'm afraid we're just having dinner.
GREY	Oh dear. I do apologise for calling at such a very inconvenient time.
PITT	Yes, you have.
GREY	But my wife and I - this is my wife -
MRS. GREY	Good evening.
GREY	We've had a slight accident with our car down your lane. I've smashed the headlights in and I really daren't go on driving in this fog. I was wondering if I could use your phone to call the A.A.
MRS. GREY	(pointedly) It's a shocking night out here - so damp and cold.
PITT	Yes - well, you must come in -
	(MRS. GREY crosses to C.)

	– for a minute or two. Do come in – for a minute or two. (He shuts the door.) I'm surprised you managed to find us: there are so few houses round here.
GREY	(going to phone) So I gathered. But you carry on with your meal. Don't let us keep you from your visitors.
PITT	Visitors? How do you know we've got visitors?
GREY	There are so many cars out there, it looks like a masonic funeral. May I use your phone right away? I'd like to get a breakdown van out here as soon as possible.
	(MELANIE comes out of the dining area as GREY starts dialling.)
PITT	Certainly. Oh, this is my wife. This lady and gentleman have had a slight accident with their car, Melanie. They've just popped in for a minute or two to use our phone.
MELANIE	I'm so glad I left the door to you, Nigel.
MRS. GREY	We haven't got the faintest idea where we are. We've been driving for hours and the weather's been getting worse all the time.
PITT	Things have been getting worse here as well, haven't they, darling?
MELANIE	Yes, we literally haven't been able to leave the house.
GREY	(on phone) Hello?..Yes.... This is .... (To PITT.) Excuse me, where am I speaking from? This phone's got no number on it.
PITT	No number on it? Oh, one of the children must've taken it out again – they're always doing that.
GREY	What is the number?

	UPROAR IN THE HOUSE	
PITT	The number? Ah, we're ex-directory, you see, and I never can remember it. (To MELANIE.) What is our number, darling?	
MELANIE	Our number? Oh, our telephone number –	
GREY	(on phone) Hold on a minute, I'm finding out.	
MELANIE	Didn't I tell you, darling? The G.P.O. came here today and changed it. Of course, I wasn't here but I think they told Miss Johansenn. Shall I go and ask her?	
GREY	I'm sure it's not necessary: just tell me where we are.	
PITT	You're in Heyford Green and this is the only house round here for miles, so you'd better arrange to meet them by your car – up the lane, not here.	
GREY	I will when I get through. (On phone.) This is Heyford Green here and we don't know the number. All I want is the local A.A. number.	
MRS. GREY	(going over to PITT) We're keeping you from your dinner. Please don't worry about us. Just carry on as if we're not here, Mr. er – Mr. –	
PITT	Pitt.	
MRS. GREY	Mr. Pitt. It's funny, I seem to have heard that name somewhere before today. And your face is defintely familiar. You're not in politics or journalism, are you?	
PITT	(aghast) Journalism? (He puts a hand to his face to shield it.) No, nothing like that at all. Come along, Melanie, we really must get things organised in the kitchen. (He crosses to MELANIE and changes hands to hide his face as he does so.) Our guests are waiting, as Mrs. –	
GREY	(at phone) Grey.	

PITT	As Mrs. Grey says. You will excuse us, won't you?
	(PITT hustles MELANIE into the kitchen, still masking his face.)
GREY	(on phone) That's not the nearest A.A. garage, surely? All right then. Can you put me through? .... Good, I'll hold on.... (To MRS. GREY.) This would happen, wouldn't it, Audrey?
MRS. GREY	Tonight of all nights. (She sits down on the tree seat, takes off one of her shoes and rubs her foot.)
	(YVONNE opens the nursery door, sticks her head out and shuts the door quickly. The noise makes MRS. GREY look up, but she is too late. At this very minute SIR LINDSAY emerges in the entrance to the dining area and hises at GREY.)
SIR LINDSAY	Psst! Psst!
GREY	(turning) Good evening.
SIR LINDSAY	Are you Carless?
GREY	I am as a matter of fact. How did you know?
SIR LINDSAY	I'm Sir Lindsay Cooper, of course. You managed to find the house all right then?
GREY	Yes. It was a bit of a job in the fog.
SIR LINDSAY	But you made it. Good man. I see you've got your camera with you.
GREY	Yes, it's very valuable, this camera.
SIR LINDSAY	Very valuable to all of us, eh? Don't you need a flashlight.
GREY	Of course I do - for night shots.
SIR LINDSAY	And you get plenty of night shots, don't you? Look out, I think someone's coming - act naturally. (He saunters stagily across the room and hises at MRS. GREY as he passes her.) I suppose you hold his

	tripod ? (To GREY.) That's our room up there, the lady and I.
GREY	The lady and you?
SIR LINDSAY	Yes. We'll try to get to bed about eleven so you can come up and take photographs of us any time after that. Good man. (He disappears back into the dining area.)
	(GREY boggles after him. MRS. GREY rises in complete disbelief.)
MRS. GREY	What on earth was he talking about?
GREY	I haven't the remotest idea. The sooner we get out of this house the better. (On phone.) Hello..... hello..... No, you can't call me back, I don't know the number. I'll call in five minutes. (He puts phone down.) They're jam-packed with calls. Goodness knows how long this is going to take. I'm awfully sorry about this, Audrey.
	(They meet U.C.)
MRS. GREY	Oh, that's all right.
	(PROSSER comes purposefully out of the au pair's suite U.L.)
PROSSER	It's no good, Miss Johansenn, I cannot stay in your room a moment longer. I must telephone Mother. Now, look here, Pitt. (He sees the GREYS.) I beg your pardon. I thought you were somebody else whom I knew, not somebody else whom I don't – that is – good evening. (He crosses over to phone.)
GREY	Good evening. If you're looking for Mr. Pitt he's in the kitchen doing something with his wife.
PROSSER	Doing something?
GREY	Yes, and I'm just phoning for help. There's been a bit of an accident.
PROSSER	An accident? This is terrible. Pitt, Pitt –

what's happened to her, Pitt? (He rushes into the kitchen in a state of great excitement.)

(MR. and MRS. GREY boggle once again. MISS JOHNSON runs out of the au pair's suite after PROSSER. As she passes the GREYS she does a double-take - who are they? - and hurries into the kitchen. YVONNE looks out of the nursery and disappears quickly again as SIR LINDSAY and LADY COOPER appear in the dining area entrance.)

SIR LINDSAY Haven't you gone yet? I thought you were going and coming back when we'd gone to bed. We don't want any smell of collusion.

GREY Collusion?!!

(There is shouting from the kitchen. PITT hurries out in a state of desperation.)

PITT (coming out) Everything's perfectly all right, Prosser, old chap. The rest of dinner's just coming, Sir Lindsay. Do go back into the dining room - please!

(SIR LINDSAY and LADY COOPER start to go but pause, fascinated by what follows.)

Did you get your call all right, Mr. - er - er? Do sit down, Mrs. er - er -

MRS. GREY (sitting in contemporary chair) Pitt. The evening paper.

PITT Evening paper?

MRS. GREY Yes, I've just recognised you - you're Nigel Pitt, aren't you?

PITT (apprehensively) Nigel Pitt - yes?

MRS. GREY (to GREY) Andrew, this is Nigel Pitt. He's just been adopted as the local Conservative candidate.

GREY Has he now? Well, I'm on the other side of the fence but nevertheless, my congratulations, Mr. Pitt.

Scene 2	UPROAR IN THE HOUSE	

PITT	(aghast) You're actually a Member of Parliament?
GREY	Yes, I may be a Labour M.P., but I've got a lot of friends who are Conservatives.
PITT	Have you?!
GREY	As a matter of fact, one of my oldest friends is your local party chairman, Sir Norman Spens.
PITT	Sir Norman? You - you know Sir Norman Spens?
GREY	Very well indeed - and Lady Spens. In fact, they're having dinner with me at the House tomorrow.
PITT	Dinner? At the House? Tomorrow?
GREY	Yes, I'm sure they'll be most interested to know we've spent the evening with you in your home - and met your charming wife.
PITT	My wife - you're going to mention my wife to Sir Norman Spens?
PROSSER	(shooting out of the kitchen) Sir Norman Spens? Did somebody say Sir Norman Spens?
GREY	Yes, I did - he's a personal friend of mine.
PITT	A personal friend!
PROSSER	But he's Chairman of the Law Society. Oh, dies infaustus - dies infaustus - I must leave here at once. (He gets to the door D.L. then remembers.) My coat!
MISS JOHNSON	(who has followed him in) I'll get it. (She hurries U.R. and disappears into the au pair's suite.)
PROSSER	(rushing after her) It's all gone much too far - we're heading for a disaster - I know we are - I can feel it. (As he reaches the stable door the upper half slams to in his face. He reels back across the stage, semi-insensible, and with a stupid grin on his face,

collapsing on his knees by MRS. GREY. He shakes hands with MRS. GREY.) I'm so sorry, madam, I didn't see you standing there.   (He shakes hands with GREY.)   Goodbye, Sir Norman, so nice to see you again.   (He shakes hands with PITT.)   Goodbye, Mr. Prosser, do give my regards to your –   (He suddenly sees MISS JOHNSON who has come back and is distraught at what she has done.) MOTHER!!   (He goes to take her in his arms but as he reaches her, he collapses again and they both tumble to the floor. PROSSER lies spread-eagled with his head against the tree seat. Going back into his childhood.)   Can I have my bread and milk now, mummy dear?

(At this very moment, MELANIE comes out of the kitchen holding a steaming saucepan of spaghetti, which she is handling with felt gloves.

MELANIE   (screaming)   David!   (She thrusts the saucepan at PITT in her anxiety.)

PITT   (juggling desperately with the hot utensil) Ooo – ah – ooo – oww – Look out!   (He dashes towards the coffee table to put the saucepan down, trips over MRS. GREY's foot and inadvertently shoots the spaghetti all over PROSSER's head and shoulders.)

QUICK CURTAIN

ACT TWO

When the curtain rises, PITT and most of his guests are discovered sitting around in the living area, while MELANIE serves them coffee from the low teak table. SIR LINDSAY is sitting on the chair D.R. LADY COOPER and MRS. GREY are sitting on the tree seat, while GREY is spread-eagled uncomfortably in the chair C. An awkward silence has fallen on the company.

MELANIE (in desperation) Would anybody like the television on?

PITT I'm not sure it's working - I mean, I'm not sure it's working properly, darling. (He switches it on. After a second smoke starts coming out of the bottom. He quickly switches it off.) Oh dear, it looks as if we've just missed 'Gunsmoke'. (He laughs and looks at his watch then returns and sits in his chair U.C.) Anyway, there's nothing left bar the Epilogue.

SIR LINDSAY Time's getting on. (To LADY COOPER.) We shall have to think of going up in a minute or two, my dear. After all tonight's excitement, I expect our host and hostess are ready for bed as well.

PITT Bed? Oh no, it's still very early by our standards. We're late birds in this house. Sometimes Melanie and I are on the go all

	night - I mean entertaining our guests like you.
GREY	It's very good of you to put us up at such short notice. If the garage do manage to come out here first thing tomorrow, we won't disturb you when we leave.
MELANIE	(rising and crossing to MRS. GREY) More coffee, Mrs. Grey?
MRS. GREY	No, thank you.
MELANIE	(returning to her chair with empty mug) I'm sorry there's such an assortment of cups but the children break everything.
PITT	Yes, things have never been quite the same since the children came on the scene.
GREY	Still, you'll find them a great advantage at election time, in spite of Sir Norman's aversion to married candidates. The family image is a great vote-catcher. I'm glad to see the old boy's come to his senses at last by selecting a married man like you, Pitt. I expect Lady Spens had something to do with that. By the way, what did you make of Sir Norman, Mrs. Pitt?
MELANIE	Sir Norman? Oh, I -
PITT	(rising and coming D.C., hastily cutting in) She hasn't actually met Sir Norman yet. Melanie prefers to stay in the background.
MRS. GREY	Don't the Conservatives interview the candidates' wives in this constituency?
PITT	No, they just judge the man on his merits. That's how I got in. It would be true to say my wife hasn't been taken into account at all - it would be quite true to say that. That's why I'd prefer you not to mention her to Sir Norman tomorrow. I'd like to effect the introduction myself.
GREY	D'you mean you've gone through the entire selection procedure without mentioning your

	wife and family? Somewhat misleading, surely?
PITT	No, I mean I was a bachelor when the selection started a few months ago, but we've got married since.
GREY	Oh, I see.
LADY COOPER	But I don't understand. You told me, Mrs. Pitt, you ran away to Gretna Green when you were twenty.
PITT	We did run away but we didn't actually get married; her father got there just in time.
SIR LINDSAY	Then how do you come to have four children, old chap? You haven't been living in – ?
PITT	No, no, of course not. They're Melanie's children by her first marriage, not mine.
LADY COOPER	I didn't realise you'd been married before, Mrs. Pitt.
MELANIE	Neither did – neither did a lot of our friends.
PITT	She married poor Geoffrey on the rebound you see, and then, when he died so tragically in the Virgin Islands, well I couldn't leave my childhood sweetheart alone with four children, could I? (Breaking L. to round behind L. side of MELANIE.)
	(MELANIE's chair is the contemporary arm chair set D.L. for the opening of ACT II.)
	I did the only thing possible. I made the supreme sacrifice and shouldered poor Geoffrey's burden for him.
MELANIE	And his burden thanks you, darling.
PITT	I didn't mean it like that, dear. (Returning to C. to collect GREY's empty mug, which he hands to MELANIE.) It's been the most rewarding period of my life to see those three – four helpless youngsters given a new start in life and forget how cruelly fate has treated them.

GREY	Most laudable of you to keep quiet about this at the present time. A lesser man would have made political capital out of something which is really just like a fairy tale.
MELANIE	Yes, isn't it?
MRS. GREY	Just how long have you two been married, Mrs. Pitt?
MELANIE	(icily) How long have we been married, darling?
PITT	Ah – how long? Well, I suppose we can't keep our little secret any longer. Actually, we only got married – er – this morning, that's it, this morning – by special licence.
	(SIR LINDSAY, LADY COOPER and MR. and MRS. GREY rise in great excitement. There is much handshaking and congratulating and kissing between the women. After general congratulations, all the ladies return to their seats.)
SIR LINDSAY	My dear fellow, I had no idea this was your wedding night. We wouldn't have dreamt of imposing on you if we'd known – let alone stayed up talking half the night –
PITT	Nonsense, Sir Lindsay, it's been most stimulating – to have you here. If you hadn't come back, Melanie and I would've been here all alone – fogbound – with nothing to do.
GREY	I really do feel most guilty about this. I've never gatecrashed a honeymoon before.
SIR LINDSAY	(quietly) Wedding photographs – not your speciality, eh? (He chuckles.)
GREY	I'm not quite sure I understand what you're talking about.
SIR LINDSAY	(quietly) Very good, very good; most convincing.
	(GREY breaks behind tree seat and joins MRS. GREY and LADY COOPER.)

ACT II UPROAR IN THE HOUSE 77

	(To PITT.) Are you sure you want to sell me this house, old chap? The circumstances must have changed since you put it on the market.
PITT	No, no, they're different but not changed. They've all been living here, you see – the children and Melanie and her mother from Ramsgate – Harrogate – my mother from Harrogate – and the house isn't big enough for us – not to mention Miss Johansenn who, as you know, has become expectant since I took her on – I mean since she married Dosser – Prosser.
SIR LINDSAY	(sitting L. end of tree seat) I thought the children had been living in this house. You can always tell.
PITT	Most definitely. You see, poor Geoffrey – I do hope this isn't distressing you to talk about it, dear?
MELANIE	No, I'm getting used to the idea now.
PITT	Poor Geoffrey was first posted missing, presumed lost, in the Virgin Islands. Then we heard definitely from the Governor of the Virgin Islands that Geoffrey had had it.
SIR LINDSAY	Had it?
PITT	Caught it.
SIR LINDSAY	Caught it?
PITT	Bought it.
GREY	(rising and making his way over to front door) So here you are with your lovely bride of twelve hours, and we're inconsiderately keeping you up. It's high time we retired for the night, Audrey. I'll fetch our bag from the car –
PITT	There's really no need to rush out. Melanie and I are in no hurry for – we've got all night for – I mean, I thought we might all have a game of poker or scrabble or – (Desperately.)

	Would you like another cup of coffee?
GREY	I wouldn't dream of it. You've done far too much for us already. I'll see you upstairs, Audrey. (He goes out D.L.)
MRS. GREY	Goodnight, Mrs. Pitt. Goodnight, Mr. Pitt. You really have been most kind to us, particularly in the circumstances. Goodnight to you. (She goes upstairs and into the bedroom extreme R.)
SIR LINDSAY	(to LADY COOPER) We'd better be toddling up as well, my dear.
LADY COOPER	Yes, we must. (She rises and starts upstairs.)
SIR LINDSAY	Don't want to keep these young people from their beauty sleep, eh, old chap? (He laughs and gives PITT a knowing wink.)
PITT	(as SIR LINDSAY goes upstairs) You're not leaving us already, are you? I was looking forward to a chat - I'm not in the least bit sleepy - I'm full of energy -
SIR LINDSAY	(from the landing) Very pleased to hear it, old chap. Goodnight, goodnight.
	(SIR LINDSAY and LADY COOPER go into the first guest room. PITT and MELANIE make their general goodnights and then wait until the bedroom door is closed.)
MELANIE	(pushing the contemporary chair back on its mark L.C.) Thank you very much, darling.
PITT	What for?
MELANIE	For marrying me off on the rebound to such a virile husband. (Crossing below PITT and sitting on tree seat.) I'm not surprised he kicked the bucket in the Virgin Islands.
PITT	I had to say something. He was suggesting the most appalling thing - that I'd been deceitful with the Selection Committee. He even implied that I, of all people, had deliberately told them a whole lot of lies.

ACT II   UPROAR IN THE HOUSE   79

MELANIE   And you never tell lies, do you, darling?

PITT   No, I do not – except when I get pitchforked
          into an impossible position with a wife I never
          wanted. I haven't done anything to deserve it.

MELANIE   No, and you're not going to get it either.

PITT   Quite frankly, Miss – Miss whatever your
          name is – I don't like the tone of your
          conversation at all.   (Breaking U.C.)
          I wish to heaven I'd never set eyes on you.

MELANIE   (rising and going to him)   So do I. I think
          you're the most self-centred, inconsiderate
          man. I've ever had the misfortune to meet. I
          come here to do a simple job and finish up on
          my honeymoon – the second one at that.

          (At this moment, PROSSER opens the top
          half of the stable door and sticks his head out.
          He overhears the last few words and is
          horrorstruck.)

PROSSER   Honeymoon? Second honeymoon?

PITT   Hello, here comes Champion the Wonder
          Horse.

PROSSER   (moving to them)   Second honeymoon? Who
          are you talking about?

PITT   Dame Sybil here.

PROSSER   This is outrageous. Have you considered the
          implications post hoc, ergo propter hoc?

MELANIE   Never mind the hoc, he's just married me off
          for the second time. Not only that, I'm
          supposed to be spending my wedding night
          with him.   (She passes below PROSSER
          to R. end of tree seat.)

PROSSER   What?

PITT   There's a very simple explanation, Prosser.
          You see, Andrew Grey was under the
          impression that Sir Norman Spens, whom I
          know and he knows, although he's on the
          other side –

PROSSER	Who is?
PITT	Grey, of course. And he was under the impression that I had misled them that I was a bachelor although I was married at the time of my selection, which, of course, I wasn't at all.
PROSSER	Wasn't you – weren't you?
PITT	Of course I weren't – wasn't. There was only one simple explanation I could give – that was that she had been married before, after I had wanted to but wasn't able to, and that the children were Geoffrey's from the Virgin Islands.
PROSSER	Virgin Islands?
PITT	Yes, Virgin Islands. So this naturally made the whole situation absolutely logical. It meant that I was telling the truth before and when I said I wasn't married I wasn't. I was only married when I was – long afterwards, this morning.
PROSSER	I don't understand a word of it, but you are not in any circumstances spending the night in the same room as my fiancee. Nor do I have any intention, as I've repeatedly told you, of compromising myself with Miss Thing in the stable.
MELANIE	(rising, crossing to PROSSER and leading him to tree seat, where they both sit) There's no need to get worked up, David. They've all gone to bed except Grey. And he's only gone to get his suitcase from the car.
PITT	(sitting L. end of tree seat) As soon as he's settled, we can all sort ourselves out for the night. Melanie can have the bedroom, I'll go in the nursery and you can bed down in the bathroom.
PROSSER	(rising) Bathroom? I can't sleep in the bathroom; it'd bring on my fibrositis.

PITT	All right then, I'll take the bathroom; there's no need to argue about it.
PROSSER	(sitting) I've never known such a night. Thank heaven I managed to phone Mother. And I hold you personally responsible Pitt. You want to remember qui facit per alium facit per se.
GREY	(coming in through the front door) He who does an act by an agent is himself responsible – which one of you does that apply to?
PITT	(rising and crossing to GREY) None of us here, of course. Prosser was just telling us about a case he's been arbitrating today. We mustn't keep you talking, Prosser, old man. I expect Helga's waiting up for you.
PROSSER	(rising and crossing to PITT) No, she isn't.
GREY	I think you and I can take a hint as men of the world, Mr. Prosser. After all, this is their very first night as Mr. and Mrs. Pitt and I can't help feeling that you and I are in the way.
PITT	(crossing to coffee table and picking up tray) In the way? Oh no, we're not going up yet. We've still got the washing up to do.
	(GREY takes tray from PITT and hands it to PROSSER. PITT clears coffee table from D.L. to below window upstage of main door.)
GREY	On your wedding night? Nonsense, my dear fellow. Miss Johansenn can take care of that in the morning. Can't she, Mr. Prosser?
PROSSER	Er, yes, er – er –
GREY	You get to bed! I'm sure Mr. Prosser will lock up for you. After you, Mrs. Pitt. (He stands at the foot of the stairs and gestures MELANIE to precede him.)
MELANIE	Oh – thank you so much. Well, goodnight,

	David. See you in the morning.
GREY	And you, Mr. Pitt
PITT	Ah, there's the central heating, you see – I must adjust the central heating – in case it turns cold in the night.
GREY	I shouldn't let that worry you. I'm sure Mr. Prosser will take care of that as well. (He gives PROSSER a hugh wink.) Won't you, Mr. Prosser?
PROSSER	Er, yes, er – er –
GREY	After you, Mr. Pitt. (He repeats the gesture.)
PITT	Yes – thank you very much. Goodnight, Prosser, old man – see you soon.
	(PROSSER sits L. end of tree seat as PITT goes up the stairs, followed by GREY. MELANIE is by now on the landing.)
GREY	(as he goes upstairs) I've been meaning to ask you about Sir Lindsay. Is he all right?
PITT	All right? What do you mean by all right?
GREY	He's said some very strange things to me tonight – very strange indeed. He seems to have an obsession about photography. He's all right in the head, is he?
PITT	I hope so – he's just bought this house.
GREY	(now at the top of the stairs) I'm sure you've got plenty of more important things on your mind right now. Goodnight to you.
	(GREY stands and looks as PITT and MELANIE go towards their room.)
PITT	Goodnight.
MELANIE	Goodnight, Mr. Grey
GREY	(still standing there) Goodnight. Sleep tight.

ACT II	UPROAR IN THE HOUSE

PITT	And you. Goodnight.
GREY	Goodnight.
PITT	Goodnight.
	(They have to go in together. The door closes. GREY turns to his room, sees PROSSER below and gives him a big wink.)
GREY	Goodnight, Mr. Prosser.
PROSSER	Yes. Thanks for your help!
	(GREY goes into his own room. The door closes. PROSSER is beside himself.)
	He's gone into her room. He's in there with her. This is outrageous. (He puts tray down on T.V. set and starts up the stairs.)
	(As he reaches the landing, SIR LINDSAY comes out of his room in pyjamas and dressing gown.)
SIR LINDSAY	Haven't you gone to bed yet, old chap? Everybody else has.
PROSSER	I'm just going.
SIR LINDSAY	But don't you sleep downstairs?
PROSSER	Yes, I do.
SIR LINDSAY	Do you want the bathroom, then? If so I'll hang on a minute.
PROSSER	No, I was just going downstairs.
SIR LINDSAY	A very goodnight to you then.
	(SIR LINDSAY leans over the bannister in a benign manner and watches PROSSER as he goes. PROSSER has to make for the au pair's suit and go inside. SIR LINDSAY surveys the empty scene, smiles and goes into the bathroom. Immediately that door closes, the au pair's door opens and PROSSER shoots out.)
PROSSER	I'm sorry, Miss Johnson. He forced me to come in here – but I kept my eyes shut.

(PROSSER starts to make for the stairs again, but now GREY comes out of his room and makes for the bathroom. PROSSER hides. He sees GREY try the door, which confirms to him that SIR LINDSAY is still in there. GREY goes back in his room again. PROSSER is momentarily undecided. Should he risk a dash upstairs or should he wait in the nursery? As always with PROSSER, caution triumphs. He goes into the nursery and closes the door. There is a moment's pause, then a stifled scream. PROSSER shoots out pursued by an irate YVONNE in her slip, clutching her dress in front of her, and a child's teddy bear.)

Good gracious, the hot potato lady. I'd forgotten.

YVONNE   How dare you come into my room in the middle of the night and grope around in the dark, you dirty old man.

PROSSER   But you don't understand, madam, I'm a solicitor and Commissioner of Oaths.

YVONNE   You'll get a few of them all right when my dad catches up with you.

PROSSER   It's not like that at all, madam. I only came into your room for necessities non habet lagem –

YVONNE   You filthy beat!   (She slaps him across the face.)

(The master bedroom door opens and PITT half emerges still fully dressed.)

PITT   (hisses)   What are you doing with that girl, Prosser? Shut her up – get her out of here.

PROSSER   You get out of there.

PITT   I'm coming now – Miss Wilby – in with Miss Johnson.

(GREY opens his door and starts to come out.

ACT II UPROAR IN THE HOUSE 85

	He calls back into his room.)
GREY	I'll see if I can get a tumbler from the bathroom, Audrey.
	(PITT has to dive back into his bedroom. YVONNE scuttles into the au pair's suite and PROSSER into the nursery. All three doors close at once. GREY makes for the bathroom. As he gets to the door, SIR LINDSAY comes out.)
SIR LINDSAY	All gone to bed, have they?
GREY	I think so.
SIR LINDSAY	We're ready when you are.
GREY	I beg your pardon?
SIR LINDSAY	She's got her nightdress on. She's all ready to be taken.
GREY	I BEG YOUR PARDON?
	(The master bedroom door opens and PITT starts to creep out. He is too late – they have seen him.)
SIR LINDSAY	Haven't you gone to bed yet, old chap?
PITT	No, I was just going to stoke the boiler – but then I remembered that Prosser had done it. Goodnight. (He goes back into the master bedroom.)
SIR LINDSAY	(starting for his room) Shy type, I think. Don't be too long, there's a good chap – she'll be getting cold. (He goes into his bedroom.)
	(GREY looks after him with a mixture of pity and astonishment. He then goes into the bathroom and closes the door. There is a fractional pause and PITT's door opens. He sticks his head out cautiously and sees that the coast is clear. He tiptoes to the bathroom and tries to open the door. At the same time, PROSSER comes out of the nursery.)
PROSSER	What have you been doing?

PITT	I've been stuck in there. I couldn't get out — I couldn't get in here.
PROSSER	I don't believe a word of it. It's outrageous, absolutely outrageous.
	(The bathroom door starts to open. PITT jumps back into his bedroom and PROSSER into the nursery. GREY walks back down the corridor carrying a tumbler. His door closes. Instantaneously, PITT's door and PROSSER's door open slowly. PITT creeps along the corridor carrying blanket and pyjamas and goes into the bathroom, watched by PROSSER. The door closes. PROSSER waits for a moment, then creeps upstairs and taps on MELANIE's door. She opens it in her nightgown.)
	You didn't let him see you like that, did you?
MELANIE	Certainly not. He's gone now and I'm going to bed. I've had quite enough for one night.
PROSSER	Mind you lock your door.
MELANIE	Why, don't you trust yourself?
PROSSER	It's not me, it's him. All the same, these politicians — say one thing and do another.
MELANIE	He's not saying or doing anything in my bedroom in the middle of the night. I maybe politically uncommitted but I'm not one of the "don't knows". Do be a good boy, David, and run along to your own room. You need a night's sleep like the rest of us.
PROSSER	Some chance of that. Pitt knew what he was doing when he gave me the nursery — it's either a cot or a four-foot bunk bed.
MELANIE	Never mind, darling. Be British: just keep a stiff upper knee. Goodnight, David. (She rewards him with a light kiss.)
	(As MELANIE is kissing PROSSER, the first guest room door opens and LADY COOPER comes out. She is taken aback by

ACT II UPROAR IN THE HOUSE 87

what she sees.)

LADY COOPER Oh, don't let me interrupt anything –

PROSSER (covered in confusion)   Oh – oh –

MELANIE David's only just found out that Nigel and I were married today. He felt he had to come up and congratulate us. Didn't you, David?

PROSSER Yes – er – oo – er –

MELANIE Wasn't that sweet of him? Give Helga a big kiss from me. Night night. (As she closes the door.)   Coming, Nigel, darling.

PROSSER (alone on the landing with LADY COOPER) Er – er – goodnight. (He rushes down the stairs in a welter of embarrassment, dashes into the nursery and locks the door.)

(LADY COOPER sees him go into the nursery, reacts, shrugs and turns to the bathroom. The bathroom door sticks momentarily, then opens. LADY COOPER goes inside. There is a strangulated male cry and, after a second, PITT rushes out in the gaudy pair of pyjamas, clutching a blanket in front of him. LADY COOPER follows him on to the landing.)

LADY COOPER What on earth are you doing in the bathroom, Mr. Pitt. Looking for floating voters?

PITT I couldn't get to sleep, you see. I was disturbing Melanie – she was disturbing me – I mean we were disturbing each other – well, to tell you the truth, I'm afraid we've had a bit of an up and a downer – a quarrel – a tiff, you know.

LADY COOPER (lapsing slightly from her pose)   Never mind, dear. As one who knows only too well, you don't want to take these things too seriously. You go back to her and make it up, love. I won't say anything.

PITT I will, Lady Cooper. You're quite right – I will – straight away – this minute – thank you –

	goodnight, Lady Cooper – (He backs up the landing in great confusion.)
LADY COOPER	(realising she has lapsed out of character) Not at all. Goodnight, Mr. Pitt. (She goes into the bathroom and closes the door.)
	(PITT tries the master bedroom door and finds it locked. At first he taps gently and then with increasing frenzy.)
PITT	Melanie – Melanie – let me in – Melanie –
	(MELANIE opens the door wearing that nightdress and looking particularly dishy.)
	(Taking her in for the first time.) Melanie!
	(SIR LINDSAY's door starts to open.)
	Look out!
	(PITT pushes past MELANIE and shuts the door. As he does so, she lets out a little scream of surprise. PROSSER's door immediately opens and he shoots out in shirt, pants, socks, suspenders and shoes. He is carrying his trousers and the birdcage and looking up in great alarm. He just misses PITT and MELANIE but is caught in mid-floor by SIR LINDSAY.)
SIR LINDSAY	What on earth d'you think you're doing, Prosser?
PROSSER	Oh – I'm just putting the bird out for the night.
SIR LINDSAY	Do you always walk about like that at night?
PROSSER	Like what? (He suddenly realises he is holding his trousers.) Oh, good gracious, what am I doing?
SIR LINDSAY	Supposing one of the ladies had – get back to your room at once –
	(PROSSER makes for the nursery.)
	– not there – your own room, man. Don't you

ACT II UPROAR IN THE HOUSE

PROSSER	(slowly going towards au pair's suite) But my trousers – I haven't got my trousers on.
SIR LINDSAY	You go and put them on if you're going to do any more night walking. There are ladies in the house. Go on.
	(PROSSER cannot escape. He has to go into the au pair's suite again. As the door closes SIR LINDSAY turns and goes back into his own room.)
	Bless my soul, the fellow must be an exhibitionist.
	(His door closes. At once, there are screams from the au pair's suite and PROSSER rushes out, pursued by YVONNE and MISS JOHNSON, both in slips. He no longer carries his trousers.)
YVONNE	How dare you do it again – you sex maniac! (She clouts him across the face.)
	(PROSSER covers his face as MISS JOHNSON squares up to him, but she kicks him on the shin. Both girls flounce back into their room and shut the door behind them, leaving PROSSER staggering back towards the nursery.
PROSSER	My trousers – I dropped my trousers in there.
	(The bathroom door opens and LADY COOPER comes out just in time to see PROSSER disappear into the nursery without his trousers. PITT hears the bathroom door open and also looks out. His reaction to the sight of PROSSER is one of even greater alarm than LADY COOPER, who goes back into her room.)
LADY COOPER	(as she goes) Goodness knows I'm broad-minded but – (The door closes.)
PITT	(into his room) Melanie, Prosser's

wandering around half naked. You don't think it's been too much for him? (He closes the door again.)

(SIR LINDSAY's door opens and he comes out.)

SIR LINDSAY (talking to LADY COOPER inside) But I just told him to put them on. I'll soon sort this out - oh, he's gone. (He goes back into his room.) If Carless doesn't come in a minute, I shall go in and fetch him out.

(The door closes. PITT, knowing the bathroom is now clear, comes out again. Gathering his blanket around him, he goes along the corridor and tries to open the bathroom door. He finds to his horror that it has now locked itself. He tries frenziedly to open it but it will not open. He goes back to the master bedroom and calls inside, hoarsely.)

PITT Darling - I mean, Melanie -

MELANIE (appearing in the doorway) What's the matter now, Nigel?

PITT I can't get in the bathroom. That lock's gone wrong again.

MELANIE You'll have to force it open then.

PITT I can't - it's jammed. Anyway, if I break it, I won't be able to lock it again. I'm in a terrible fix. I've got nowhere to sleep at all now - and I'm tired and I want to go to bed.

MELANIE The only room that isn't occupied or locked is the kitchen -

PITT Have a heart. Can you see me bedding down on a strip of Formica? I know, I'll go to the garage and sleep in the car.

MELANIE You can't do that in pyjamas, Nigel, you'll catch your death of cold. Where are your clothes?

ACT II　　　　UPROAR IN THE HOUSE

PITT
: Locked in the bathroom.

MELANIE
: Back to that again. There's only one thing for it. I'll make you up a bed on the couch.

PITT
: I can't sleep down there. Anybody can see me there.

MELANIE
: No, the studio couch, in here.

PITT
: What? I can't do that – all night in there with you?

MELANIE
: Why – what's the matter with me?

PITT
: Nothing – nothing at all – that's the trouble. (Hastily.) Not that I –

MELANIE
: I never thought you would. You're not like that, are you?

PITT
: No, no I'm not – at least, I don't think so. But what's Prosser going to say?

MELANIE
: He's not going to say anything. He thinks you're in the bathroom and I'm not going to disillusion him.

PITT
: I suppose if I was out of the room early no one need be any the wiser.

MELANIE
: Of course not. They're all sound asleep now. Come on. (She goes inside.)

PITT
: I hope to heaven Central Office never hear about this. What would they think with a slogan like "Action – not words"? (He switches the lights off from the landing, goes in and closes the door.)

(There is a pause and then a jangling of keys at the front door as the PHOTOGRAPHER lets himself in with a master key. He quietly closes the door, looks round the room and then creeps up the stairs. He stops outside the bathroom and listens without result. Now he comes to the master bedroom and listens with an ear to the door. He obviously hears voices because he straightens up, reacts and then listens again. Gently, he tries the door handle but it is locked. This surprises him slightly, so he listens again. What he hears obviously convinces him. Holding his camera high, he kicks open the door, dashes inside and takes a flashlight photograph. MELANIE immediately begins to scream and PITT starts shouting. Realising his mistake, the PHOTOGRAPHER dashes out, ducks down the stairs and goes straight out through the front door which closes behind him. PITT and MELANIE come rushing out on to the landing in their night attire as do SIR LINDSAY and LADY COOPER and the GREYS simultaneously: and PROSSER, still without his trousers, from the nursery. As the climax mounts, MISS JOHNSON appears in the au pair's doorway with YVONNE cowering behind her.)

GREY
What the devil's going on?

PITT
A photograph - somebody took a photograph.

MRS. GREY
A photograph?

MELANIE
Yes, a flashlight photograph in our room.

PROSSER
(almost beside himself) They were together - they were together.

SIR LINDSAY
(rounding on GREY) You blithering idiot, you've taken the wrong couple.

PITT
He's taken the wrong couple? (He dashes downstairs on noticing YVONNE and shoos her back into the au pair's suite.)

GREY
Don't look at me: I didn't have anything to do with it, whatever he - (He gestures to SIR LINDSAY.) - may say.

SIR LINDSAY
Do you mean it wasn't you?

GREY
Of course it wasn't me. D'you think I make a habit of charging into people's bedrooms and taking flashlight photographs in the middle of the night?

ACT II	UPROAR IN THE HOUSE	93
SIR LINDSAY	Don't you?	
GREY	Of course I don't. (Thumping down the stairs.) I ought to sue you for suggesting it. I am a professional politician, a Member of Parliament. How dare you infer I'd allow myself to be involved in something completely distasteful and unprincipled.	
PITT	It's worse for me – at least you're a Socialist. You don't seem to realise my position. Somebody's just run out of this house with a negative showing Melanie and me in a highly compromising situation.	
PROSSER	He admits – he's standing there admitting it. Flagrante delicto.	
PITT	You keep Flagrante delicto out of this. It's got nothing to do with you.	
PROSSER	It's got everything to do with me –	
PITT	Here am I, the parliamentary candidate for this constituency and my whole reputation is at stake.	
	(PROSSER sits on the tree seat.)	
GREY	Don't be such a damn fool, man. How can you be compromised with your own wife?	
PITT	You can't – that's just it – and that's not all – because I'm not – (Faltering.) – we're not – (Lamely.) – anyway, it's not nice.	
GREY	And it's not very nice for me to be mixed up in this sort of thing either. I don't know what's going on in this house and I don't want to know. I'm going back to my bed and I shall make a point of seeing my wife and I leave as soon as it's daylight. Come along, Audrey. (He starts up the stairs followed by MRS. GREY.)	
MRS. GREY	Goodnight once again, everyone. (To GREY.) I do think you're making rather a fuss over nothing, Andrew. After all, it's not as if they took a photograph of us, is it?	
	(They go into their bedroom and close the door.)	

LADY COOPER	Is that man really a Member of Parliament?
PITT	(highly agitated) Of course he is. And what's even worse, he knows Sir Norman and Lady Spens.
MELANIE	He knows Sir Norman and Lady Spens?
PROSSER	Yes, he knows Sir Norman and Lady Spens.
	(MELANIE goes into master bedroom.)
SIR LINDSAY	Who are Sir Norman and Lady Spens?
PROSSER	(rising and crossing to SIR LINDSAY, who is D.L.) Don't you know Sir Norman and Lady Spens?
SIR LINDSAY	I've never heard of Sir Norman or Lady Spens.
PROSSER	But Sir Norman Spens is on the council of the Law Society.
PITT	(coming D.R. of PROSSER, realisation dawning) So he is. I'd forgotten that – no wonder you knocked yourself out. Did I gather from your comments just now this situation was something to do with you, Prosser
PROSSER	No, it's not. It's nothing to do with me – I don't want to be associated with it at all. In the words of Horace, mea virtute me involve – I wrap myself in my integrity.
PITT	I'm glad to see you've put your trousers on first.
SIR LINDSAY	Quite right. I think we've had enough ugly scenes for one night. I would suggest, Mr. Prosser, that in view of your wife's delicate condition you should both get back into bed at once.
PITT	(throwaway) After a couple of suitable quotations, of course.
MISS JOHNSON	(coming out of the nursery and making for the au pair's suite) Is really no need to concern yourself, Sir Lindsay. I am very robust.

SIR LINDSAY	All the more reason for taking good care of yourself. (He starts for stairs.)	

(MISS JOHNSON goes into the au pair's suite.)

I'm sorry you've had this unfortunate experience Pitt, but instinct tells me you have absolutely no cause for alarm.

PITT You wouldn't say that if you knew all I know about what you don't - that is - goodnight.

SIR LINDSAY Goodnight. I'm sure you'll find in the morning the whole things has been a complete mistake.

PITT I don't need to wait till the morning.

SIR LINDSAY Are you coming, my dear?

LADY COOPER (starting upstairs) I certainly am. I never dreamt things were going to turn out like this.

SIR LINDSAY (going upstairs) I'm sorry I've put up such a black with Grey, but I did ask him if he was him and he said he was. But if he isn't, then where the hell is he?

LADY COOPER Not far away if he's like most of them.

(They go into their room and the door closes.)

PROSSER (to PITT) Him - them - what are they talking about?

(MELANIE comes out of master bedroom, listening, and comes downstairs.)

And what were you doing in Melanie's bedroom in the first place?

PITT I wasn't doing anything in the first place - or the second place either.

MELANIE (coming between PITT and PROSSER) You don't understand, David, I was only putting Nigel to bed.

PROSSER Putting him to bed? Do you know what you're saying?

PITT Keep your voice down. We don't want everyone in the house to hear. I'd got nowhere else to

	sleep because I couldn't get in the bathroom.
PROSSER	(shouts) But you were in the bathroom – (Whispers.) I saw you go in there.
PITT	I know, but I had to come out. Then when I tried to get in again, I couldn't. So Melanie let me in.
PROSSER	You didn't do that, did you, Melanie? You'd no right to let him in.
MELANIE	I've every right to do as I please if I feel like it.
PROSSER	(breaking to D.R. of tree seat) You've no right to feel like it. You're engaged to me and –
PITT	(following him) Will you keep your voice down?
PROSSER	What do you expect me to think when I saw you coming unashamedly out of her bedroom? It made my blood boil – I could think of only one thing, one thing. Virgil, I thought, Virgil –
MELANIE	(coming D.C.) Virgil?
PROSSER	(crossing below PITT to her) Yes – Virgil's tag, the one that says quod fieri debet praesumitur esse factum.
MELANIE	What's that mean?
PROSSER	What ought to have been done is presumed to have been done.
MELANIE	Charming. I'm just beginning to realise, David, what a thoroughly unpleasant mind you have.
PITT	And before we have any more insinuations, I've got a maxim for you: tuus res agitur paries si proximus ardet.
PROSSER	I beg your pardon?
PITT	Your property is only in jeopardy if your neighbour's party wall is on fire.

ACT II	UPROAR IN THE HOUSE	97

PROSSER: Well, I'm not having my property in jeopardy any longer.

MELANIE: (crossing L.) Your property? I like that. Anyone would think I was an old boot -

PITT: (following her, quietly) Don't raise your voice like that. (Almost shouting.) You'll have them all out again.

PROSSER: I don't care if they do come out. I've had about as much as I can stand.

PITT: And I've had about as much as I can stand of you, Prosser. The law is an ass all right - and you're it. Will you get it into your tiny mind, once and for all, I do not have designs upon your fiancee. I admit I find her extremely attractive, amusing, intelligent and sympathetic - all the virtues one would least expect to find in a woman - but she's engaged to you and that's an end to it - a pretty dull end from her point of view, but I accept it. (Breaking upstage.)

PROSSER: I'm not accepting anything. (Crossing to MELANIE.) Melanie, I expect you to transfer your things from the main bedroom to the nursery at once.

PITT: (coming downstage) Just a minute, I'm not having a change of bowling at the nursery end tonight.

PROSSER: Don't be so ridiculous, I've told you before I'm a Rotarian - and an Oddfellow.

PITT: You can say that again.

PROSSER: (circular movement below PITT to C.) I'm not staying in the nursery as well - the idea of it! I'm coming up with you - where I can keep an eye on you.

PITT: That's all I need, Prosser - a night with you in a circular bed.

(MISS JOHNSON appears from au pair suite trying to quieten them.)

PROSSER	And another thing: would somebody please tell that frenzied hot potato lady I have no intention of molesting her whatsoever.
PITT	Molesting her what?
PROSSER	Her whatsoever! You're at it again – twisting everything I say.
PITT	All right, there's no need to get excited about it.
PROSSER	I've every right to get excited – every right. How would you like to find your fiancee usurped by another man and then be foisted off with the first – the first pregnant Swede available.
MISS JOHNSON	Don't you speak about me like that. I wouldn't be available to you if you were the last man on earth – the very last man.
	(The first guest room door opens and SIR LINDSAY comes out on to the landing.)
SIR LINDSAY	I don't want to appear unreasonable, but would you please all go to bed? It's quite impossible for us to sleep with all this noise going on.
PITT	(feigned surprise) Did we disturb you, Sir Lindsay? Prosser was just telling us about some of the strange things he gets up to when he finds it hard to arbitrate – pass judgement.
SIR LINDSAY	Surely it can keep till the morning? Do come up now, there's a good chap.
PITT	We will, we're coming right away. After you, darling.
	(MELANIE starts up the stairs.)
	Goodnight, Helga – goodnight, Prosser. See you again very soon.
PROSSER	You certainly will.
PITT	Goodnight, Sir Lindsay. I do assure you this is normally a very peaceful house – almost deserted, isn't it darling?

ACT II UPROAR IN THE HOUSE 99

       (PROSSER climbs on to tree seat and tries to climb up tree.)

MELANIE   Yes, it is darling. Goodnight, Sir Lindsay.
SIR LINDSAY   Goodnight - goodnight.
PITT   )
MELANIE) (together)   Goodnight.

       (They go into their room and close the door.)

SIR LINDSAY   Goodnight, Mrs. Prosser. Do go to bed and get the sleep you need in your delicate condition - (He notices PROSSER.) - and take Tarzan with you.

MISS JOHNSON   I will. Come, David. Goodnight, Sir Lindsay.

SIR LINDSAY   Goodnight - goodnight.   (He watches them go towards the au pair's suite and then goes back into his room. As he closes the door:) I've got them out of the way. I'll give them a minute and then find Carless. (The door closes.)

       (The door to the au pair's suite opens and YVONNE's voice is heard.)

YVONNE   (off) I'm not having him in here - I'm not having him in here.

PROSSER   (coming out) My good woman, I've told you before I'm a practising solicitor not Jack the Ripper. (Closing the door.) Oh, what a night - what a night. (He scuttles down to the nursery and goes inside for his things.)

       (As the nursery door closes, the master bedroom door opens and PITT looks out.)

PITT   It's all clear. I'll go down and get Prosser up.

MELANIE   (appearing at doorway) There's no need to be in such a hurry, Nigel. After all, this is our wedding night. (She puts her arms round his neck and kisses him, and then goes back into her room, closing the door.)

PITT   (reacting slowly) I say - good Lord! (He

	turns in his tracks and hurries back into the master bedroom.)
	(PROSSER comes out of the nursery with his things and goes upstairs to the master bedroom. He tries to open the bedroom door and finds it locked. This sends him into a fury and he rattles it noisily.)
PROSSER	Open this door at once. I insist upon seeing what's going on.
	(SIR LINDSAY comes out of his bredroom, sees PROSSER and reacts in amazement.)
SIR LINDSAY	What on earth do you think you're doing?
PROSSER	Oh - I - I want the bathroom. I must have the bathroom.
SIR LINDSAY	Do you usually talk to people in the bathroom like that? Anyway, that's not the bathroom: the bathroom's next door.
PROSSER	Is it? Oh, dear, how silly of me. (He tries the bathroom door but, of course, it will not open.) There must be someone in there. I'll have to find something else - I mean go somewhere else - I mean - (He rushes down the stairs covered in embarrassment. He makes for the nursery and is about to go in.)
SIR LINDSAY	Not in there - that's the nursery. What's the matter, man, are you drunk or desperate?
PROSSER	No, no, certainly not. (He careers up the steps into the au pair's suite.)
	(As the door closes, a female cry is heard. SIR LINDSAY watches him go and shakes his head.)
SIR LINDSAY	Expectant fathers - all the same.
	(The master bedroom door opens and PITT sticks his head out.)
	Great heavens above, haven't you gone to bed yet? You must be the slowest bridegroom on

ACT II UPROAR IN THE HOUSE 101

record.

PITT   Slow but sure. Goodnight, Sir Lindsay. Goodnight.
SIR LINDSAY   Goodnight.
PITT   Goodnight.

(The master bedroom door closes. SIR LINDSAY looks round and then hurries down the stairs. He crosses to the front door, unlocks it, and goes out leaving it slightly ajar.)

SIR LINDSAY   (as he goes) Carless. Are you there, Carless? (He disappears upstage outside.)

(After a short pause, the PHOTOGRAPHER appears from the opposite direction and comes in. He is crossing towards the stairs when PROSSER shoots out of the au pair's suite. His entrance causes the PHOTOGRAPHER to duck into the kitchen. PROSSER is about to enter the nursery, when he notices the front door is open. He hurries across, closes and locks it, and hurries back into the nursery. As the nursery door closes, the letter box flap lifts and SIR LINDSAY calls hoarsely through.)

Mrs. Hamilton. Mrs. Hamilton. Mrs. Hamilton!

(There is no reply. The flap closes, and SIR LINSDAY is seen, through the open venetian blinds, making his way round the house in his pyjamas. PROSSER comes out of the nursery just as the PHOTOGRAPHER starts to come out of the kitchen. The latter quickly disappears again without being seen. PROSSER creeps up the stairs and has just reached PITT's door when there is a commotion from the au pair's suite and SIR LINDSAY is hustled out by YVONNE.

YVONNE   How dare you muck about with my french window like that. (She clouts him across the

SIR LINDSAY	(as she goes) But I was locked out Miss – Miss –
	(The door slams.)
	Who's she? What are they doing with a young girl in there?
	(As SIR LINDSAY starts up the stairs, he sees PROSSER outside PITT's door once again, trying to get in.)
	Good God, Prosser, not again!
PROSSER	I can't wait any longer – I can't stop down there doing nothing.
SIR LINDSAY	I've told you before, the bathroom's next door.
PROSSER	Is it? Oh, yes – right – that's it, then. (In his confusion he wrestles frantically with the bathroom handle, manages to force open the door and hurtles inside. The door closes.)
	(The master bedroom door opens again and PITT looks out.)
PITT	Oh – oh, oh – goodnight.
SIR LINDSAY	Merciful heaven, he's still thinking about it. (He pads down the corridor and taps on the door of the GREYs' room.)
GREY	(off, as the door opens) Come in.
SIR LINDSAY	I'm terribly sorry to disturb you, but I do feel I owe you an apology. I really did think earlier this evening that you were someone else. (He goes into the room and the door closes.)
	(There is a pause and the PHOTOGRAPHER comes out of the kitchen. He views the deserted scene and then makes for the stairs carrying his camera. He has only just started the ascent, when the bathroom door opens and PROSSER comes out. The PHOTOGRAPHER immediately jumps for

(Sir Lindsay's first line begins: "face and goes back into the room.)")

ACT II UPROAR IN THE HOUSE

cover. Now the GREYs' door opens and SIR LINDSAY comes out just in time to see PROSSER actually disappearing into PITT's bedroom.)

(Shaking his head.) I don't care any more. I just don't care. (He goes into his own room and shuts the door.)

(The PHOTOGRAPHER comes out and is about to climb the stairs again when PITT's door opens and PITT looks out. The PHOTOGRAPHER jumps into the dining area.)

PITT (into the room) It's all right, darling, there's no one about.

PROSSER (off) Don't keep calling her darling.

PITT (as MELANIE comes out carrying blankets and clothes) It's only a figure of speech. (To her, quietly.) And a very pretty figure as well.

(MELANIE gives PITT a quick kiss and hurries down the stairs.)

PROSSER (off) What was that - what went on?

PITT Nothing - nothing at all.

MELANIE (going down the staircase) He's getting absolutely impossible.

PITT Never mind, I'll see he's no more trouble tonight.

MELANIE (now C. and looking up at PITT on the balcony) Romeo, Romeo, wherefore art thou, Romeo?

PITT (pointing dramatically) Get thee to a nunnery - a nursery.

(MELANIE blows him a kiss and goes off D.R.)

PROSSER (off) What are you playing at now?

PITT As You Like It. (He switches off the lights and the stage is in semi-darkness once again.) We'd better toss for it: heads I have the bed, tails you have the couch.

(The master bedroom door closes. All is now quiet. The PHOTOGRAPHER comes out of the dining area and at last makes his way up the stairs. He obviously knows where he is going this time – it is straight to the GREYs' room. He checks his camera, listens and then bursts into the room. There is a flash from inside and then pandemonium breaks out. The PHOTOGRAPHER tears down the stairs and spins round – he has momentarily lost his bearings – and then dashes into the au pair's suite. As soon as he opens the door, MISS JOHNSON and YVONNE start screaming at the tops of their voices. The PHOTOGRAPHER runs out and makes for the nearest alternative – the nursery. MELANIE's screams send him running straight out again. At this moment, all the upstairs doors start to open and the PHOTOGRAPHER is caught R.C. There is no time for him to escape: he does the only thing possible – he jumps into the well between the seat and the tree and lies low under the blanket lying across it. GREY, MRS. GREY, SIR LINDSAY and LADY COOPER emerge from their respective rooms. PITT and PROSSER come out of the master bedroom, MELANIE from the nursery and MISS JOHNSON and YVONNE from the au pair's suite. They react severally and together.)

PITT	What's going on? What's the matter now? What's all the noise about?
GREY	Who did that – who took that photograph?
MRS. GREY	It's somebody here – it must be somebody here.
SIR LINDSAY	(seeing MELANIE) What's she doing down there? And Prosser, what are you doing up here, in there with him?
PROSSER	Oh, homo homini lupus.
PITT	Be quiet, you hot-blooded Latin.
MELANIE	Yes, shut up, David, shut up!

GREY	(stomping down the stairs with the others following him) I'm going to get to the bottom of this. Nobody comes into my room and starts taking photographs without explanation.	
MRS. GREY	Do be careful, Andrew.	
	(By now GREY is downstairs and the others are following.)	
GREY	(seeing YVONNE for the very first time) Who are you? What are you doing here? I've never seen you before. Have you got a camera?	
YVONNE	No, I haven't and I haven't got nothing else left either. That Mr. Pitt's had me – hidden away for hours and I've had enough of it. I've been intruded with by him – (She points to SIR LINDSAY.) – and by him – (She points to PROSSER.) – three times. And all I've had for me trouble is two hot potatoes in me hand – and I had to grab them while I could.	
PITT	(pulling himself together) Now, now, Yvonne, we know you're still inclined to imagine things after your unfortunate experience with that Co-operative milkman – that over co-operative Co-operative milkman – but you really must forget all about it and go back to bed.	
GREY	Hold on a minute. Just who is this young lady and what have you been doing to her, Pitt?	
PITT	I haven't done anything except give her board and lodging. She ran away from home recently and we found her and took her in.	
YVONNE	You can say that again! It's lies, all lies – every single word of it. I've had as much as I can stand – being intruded upon by men all over the place. (She crosses down to telephone, followed by PITT.) I'm going to ring up me Dad again, but this time I'll tell him the truth. He'll soon get me out of this den of inequality.	
PITT	(taking her back U.C., desperately) There's no need for that, Yvonne. He knows you've been in good hands here – that is, he knows	

	you're quite safe with us. You mustn't go getting him up in the middle of the night.
YVONNE	He won't have to get up. He's up already.
PITT	Up already? What do you mean?
YVONNE	He's on night duty this week: station sergeant.
PITT	Do you mean to tell me your father is a - (Gulp.) - policeman?
YVONNE	Yeah. He'll sort you lot out quick enough. They don't call him Truncheon-Happy Wilby for nothing.
PITT	We can't have the police in here.
SIR LINDSAY	No, it's out of the question.
PITT	Why haven't you mentioned him before?
YVONNE	You've never asked me, have you? You never even noticed me in the office. All those months I spent in that little room duplicating like crazy from morning till night, and what did I get for it? Two quid a week and inky fingers. I'm fed up with being ignored, unwanted, a nobody. (She starts to cry.) I want to have a gay, worthwhile, intelligent life like - Marianne Faithfull. (She collapses on upstage L. end of tree seat. A great wail follows and she sobs uncontrollably.)
PITT	That's all we need now: the psychedelic daughter of Dixon of Dock Green. Somebody get her out of here.
MELANIE	(crossing to YVONNE with MISS JOHNSON) Why don't you leave the poor little thing alone? (Comforting her.) What harm has she done you?
MISS JOHNSON	Yes, you've done nothing but - I mean, you have nothings done but pick upon her ever since she was supposed not to be here.
MELANIE	I've never seen grown men behave like it. You ought to be ashamed of yourselves -

		particularly you, David.
PROSSER		(pushed C. by the rest of the men) Me? This is reductio ad absurdum – quite ad absurdum. Thank heaven Mother can't hear you now. I'm innocent of all the charges.
YVONNE		(turning on him) Oh, no you're not. You're the worst of the lot – you and your filthy foreign language. (Another great wail.) My dad'll book the lot of you for abdicating me.
PROSSER		(breaking down to in front of contemporary chair L.C.) I'm innocent, I tell you, innocent. What's more, I reserve my defence!
PITT		Sit down, Prosser, sit down! (He pushes him down on to the chair C.)
MRS. GREY		(crossing to GREY C.) I'd say we've heard quite enough, Andrew. I don't think we should stay here a minute longer – car or no car.
GREY		(motioning her to the stairs) You're right, Audrey. If ever anyone was keeping a disorderly house, this is it. We'll get our things at once.
		(They start up the stairs. MRS. GREY goes first, GREY following.)
LADY COOPER		(crossing to SIR LINDSAY's L.) I don't think we want to get involved with the police ourselves, do we, Sir Lindsay – in the circumstances?
SIR LINDSAY		No, you're quite right, my dear, we don't. I think we'd better make tracks as well.
PITT		(aghast) Make tracks? Leave? What about the house? You can't let me down at the last minute.
SIR LINDSAY		(leading him downstage by the arm: sotto voce) It's got nothing to do with the house, old chap. You see, it's Lady Cooper, she's not.
PITT		Not what?

SIR LINDSAY	Lady Cooper. (He whispers.) She's not my wife, old chap. Strictly between ourselves, she's a professional co-respondent.
PITT	(loudly, aghast) A co-respondent? Lady Cooper is a professional co-respondent?
MELANIE	She's a professional what?
PROSSER	Oh, proh prudor! What would Mother say? I've shared my spaghetti with a professional co-respondent.
PITT	(pushing him down yet again) Sit down, Prosser!
GREY	(coming out of his room) What's all this? Who's a professional co-respondent?
PITT	That woman there.
LADY COOPER	Don't you call me that woman.
SIR LINDSAY	(going to him) Yes, steady on, old chap.
GREY	(from the balcony) Well, what is going on here?
PITT	(making up the stairs) I'll tell you what's going on here. He's brought that wo - that lady into my house, passed her off as his wife, and all he wanted to do was commit - to provide grounds for - (Now up on the landing.) My God, he had no intention of buying this house at all!
SIR LINDSAY	(looking up at him) That's just where you're wrong, old chap. I have every intention of buying this house.
PITT	(making as if to return down the stairs) That's different then.
GREY	(stopping him) It isn't different at all. You can't condone this sort of thing for financial gain.
MELANIE	He's not condoning it. He's just saying it's different.
PITT	Yes, I'm just saying it's different.

ACT II UPROAR IN THE HOUSE 109

(MRS. GREY appears in the second guest room doorway.)

GREY It's morally indefensible. This house is nothing more nor less than a cesspool.

MELANIE Charming, I must say.

GREY Hidden photographers, professional adulterers.

LADY COOPER How dare you!

GREY Slimy solicitors –

PROSSER Good gracious!

GREY Teenage girls held in bedrooms. Goodness knows what elese has been going on here.

YVONNE I think I'm going to faint!

PITT Then put your head between your knees, you haven't got far to go.

MISS JOHNSON Quick – outside. (She hustles YVONNE into the au pair's suite.)

PROSSER I think I'm going to faint, too.

SIR LINDSAY (pushing him down) No, you're not. Sit down, Prosser.

GREY As a Labour M.P. I've witnessed some pretty shady things in my time –

PITT (starting down the stairs) As a Conservative I'm not surprised to hear it.

GREY (pursuing him with MRS. GREY following him) You'll regret that remark, Pitt. Wait until I see Sir Norman Spens tomorrow – I shall tell him that his local candidate shared his wedding night with another man.

PROSSER (starting to rise) Oh, homo homini lupus.

GREY (coming up behind him) Yes, pansies among the lupins. I told Lord Arran what it would lead to. Sit down, Prosser!

PROSSER (jumping up like a jack-in-the-box between MELANIE and PITT) This is the last straw.

110   UPROAR IN THE HOUSE   ACT II

        Stand up, Prosser. I will not be muzzled a minute longer.

MISS JOHNSON (coming in from au pair's suite) She feels better now.

PROSSER I don't, I feel worse. I was in his room – (He taps PITT on the chest.) – because I'm not having him alone with her – (He almost taps MELANIE on the chest.) Oh, dear – with her when she's going to marry me.

MELANIE Don't count your chickens, David.

SIR LINDSAY (crossing to L. of GREY) Marry you? But you can't marry her – she's married to him. (Pointing to PITT.) And you're married to Miss Johansenn from Sweden.

MISS JOHNSON (moving D.R.) From Sweden be blowed. I'm from Swiss Cottage.

SIR LINDSAY Swiss Cottage?

PROSSER (crossing to SIR LINDSAY D.L.) Yes, you've got it all wrong. Melanie's not married to him at all.

MRS. GREY Not married to him? But what about the children?

GREY Yes, they've got four children.

SIR LINDSAY Do you mean they've got four little ba – four little – ?

MELANIE No, no, no. There aren't any children, Sir Lindsay.

PROSSER No! And what's more I'm not married to Miss Swedish Cottage either.

SIR LINDSAY (crossing to MISS JOHNSON D.R.) You're not married? Then she must be expecting a little ba – what is she expecting?

MISS JOHNSON This is too much. I can't bear it. (She begins to weep and rushes out into the au pair suite.)

        (MELANIE follows her.)

ACT II — UPROAR IN THE HOUSE

PITT: She's not expecting anything except the sack when Lockwood finds out what's been going on here.

LADY COOPER: It was never like this in the best London hotels.

GREY: Lockwood? Who the devil's Lockwood?

PITT: He's my employer. The whole thing was his fault — he made me do it.

GREY: Disgraceful — absolutely disgraceful.

PITT: I know. But faced with his ultimatum, there was only one answer I could give — only one thing I could say. Mr. Lockwood, I said — (Looking into the seat round the tree.) — who the hell are you?

SIR LINDSAY: What did you say to him, old chap?

PITT: Who the hell are you?

GREY: What did you say that for?

PITT: Not to Lockwood. I'm talking to him in there. Who the hell are you?

(The PHOTOGRAPHER rises slowly like a phoenix from the ashes and politely raises his hat. He is a seedy, mournful little man in his thirties with a shock of hair, a weedy moustache, and is wearing a greasy trench coat.)

PHOTOGRAPHER: Good evening — good morning —

PITT:) The photographer!
MRS. GREY:) That's him, that's the one!
SIR LINDSAY:) Goodness me, it's Carless.
GREY:) This is a scandal, a public scandal.
LADY COOPER:) More troube — more trouble.

PROSSER: Oh, good gracious! Sit down, Prosser! (He sits.)

PITT: (grabbing the PHOTOGRAPHER by the lapels

	and hauling him out from the tree) So you're the man who had the effrontery to break into my bedroom –
GREY	And ours as well. How dare you!
PITT	Do you realise you could end up in court for this?
PHOTOGRAPHER	That is the object of the exercise, sir. The divorce court, to be precise, or as my good lady always refers to it – the breaker's yard. I'm a private inquiry agent. (He releases himself from PITT's grasp with a deft judo move.)
	(PITT subsides on to tree seat.)
	Do you mind, sir? It may not look much to you, but it's seen me through many a dirty weekend – speaking meteorologically, of course.
SIR LINDSAY	(crossing to PHOTOGRAPHER) I feel I owe you all an apology. Mr. Carless is here on my behalf. How do you do, Mr. Carless. I'm Sir Lindsay Cooper.
PHOTOGRAPHER	(nonplussed) Sir Lindsay Cooper? Yes – very pleased to meet you, sir.
	(He shakes hands; SIR LINDSAY winces.)
MELANIE	(hurrying in from the au pair's suite) Has anybody got any brandy? (She sees the PHOTOGRAPHER.) Good evening.
PHOTOGRAPHER	Good evening, madam.
MELANIE	(double take) Just a minute, who are you?
LADY COOPER	This is Mr. Carless of Carless and Greene who seems to have photographed everyone here tonight except my client.
MISS JOHNSON	(swaying in the doorway to the au pair's suite) Brandy! (She goes again.)
LADY COOPER	(to MELANIE) Come on. (As they hurry upstairs.) I've got a flask of brandy in my

ACT II UPROAR IN THE HOUSE 113

	case. I've always carried one ever since I had a brigadier pass out on me.
	(The telephone rings briefly.)
MELANIE	I'll take it in the bedroom. (She goes into the first guest room with LADY COOPER and closes the door.)
SIR LINDSAY	Sorry about all this confusion, Mr. Carless.
PHOTOGRAPHER	(crossing to C.) Well, you can't win them all, sir. Only the other day I had a very delicate case, a divorce court judge as a matter of fact – and he lost as well.
PITT	You mean he exercised his discretion once too often?
PHOTOGRAPHER	Exactly so, sir.
GREY	(spinning him round and grabbing him by the lapels) Never mind the small talk. What about those photographs you took in my room? What's happened to them, eh?
PHOTOGRAPHER	(sagging by the lapels) I'm sorry, sir. I'm afraid I don't recognise you in the vertical instead of the horizontal. What did you say your name was?
GREY	(shaking the PHOTOGRAPHER violently) Never mind who I am. I want those photographs you took destroyed or handed over to me at once.
PHOTOGRAPHER	(freeing himself with another quick judo move) I do wish you wouldn't do that, sir.
MELANIE	(appearing on the balcony with LADY COOPER behind her) I don't want to interrupt anything, but that call was for you, Sir Lindsay.
SIR LINDSAY	For me?
MELANIE	Yes, it was your Mr. Carless. He says he's stuck at Haywards Heath and he won't be able to get here to do the job tonight.
SIR LINDSAY	Good gracious!

PITT	That was Carless on the phone?
MELANIE	That's what I said, darling.
PITT	But if that was Carless on the phone, who the hell are you? (Grabbing PHOTOGRAPHER by the lapels.) You said you were Carless.
PHOTOGRAPHER	No, I didn't sir. The lady said I was Carless.
PITT	(shaking him) Never mind who said it. Who are you? What are you doing in my house?
PHOTOGRAPHER	Getting slightly fed up with being treated like a pepper pot.
	(He slips out of the raincoat, leaving PITT holding it by the lapels. He then takes the coat from PITT and elbows him in the stomach at the same time. PITT collapses on the tree seat, picks up the PHOTOGRAPHER's flattened camera and hands it to him.)
PITT	Now look what you've done to your camera.
MELANIE	(reaching the bottom of the stairs with LADY COOPER) I do wish you'd leave my husband alone.
GREY	Yes, it's disgraceful. Who the hell do you think you are?
PHOTOGRAPHER	(going to him) I'm afraid this is going to come as a bit of a shock to you, sir. My name is Prendergast and I am retained in this instance by Croxley Sons and Witchett, solicitors.
PROSSER	Croxley Sons and Witchett? I've used their Chambers!
PHOTOGRAPHER	Yes, they are acting on the instructions of your wife, sir.
GREY	) My wife?
PITT	) His wife?
SIR LINDSAY	) I say!
LADY COOPER	) His wife?
PROSSER	) His wife, yes.

PHOTOGRAPHER	Yes, sir. I am here on behalf of the real Mrs. Grey, the one in Hampstead Garden Suburb - not the charming lady present on this occasion. (Breaking upstage.)
MRS. GREY	(backing towards the stairs) Oh - oh, dear.
PITT	(cutting over) But if she's not his wife, what's he been doing here with her?
MELANIE	Well, he hasn't been making a maiden speech, darling. Wait until Sir Norman Spens hears about this.
GREY	But this is not true. (He makes for the stairs.) I'm not staying here to have my reputation besmirched.
MRS. GREY	It's no good blustering, Andrew. Mr. Prendergast obviously knows what he's talking about.
MISS JOHNSON	(appearing pathetically U.R.) Can I have some brandy, please?
LADY COOPER	Here you are. (She goes out U.R. with MISS JOHNSON.)
PHOTOGRAPHER	(crossing to the GREYs) I'm afraid that since the Government was returned with such a large majority, sir, your wife has become increasingly suspicious of your all-night sittings.
PITT	She must have known you were lying in more ways than one.
GREY	Blast you, Prendergast, blast my wife, and blast the lot of you. You don't seem to understand this lady and I had a very special relationship. She's a Member of Parliament as well.
PITT	Liberal, I suppose?
GREY	How dare you! I'm warning you. I'll - I'll -
PHOTOGRAPHER	(cutting over and coming downstage to main door) Yes, well, I think I'll be getting along now. The lady I'm cohabiting with this week

	will have my breakfast ready. Good morning, all. I'll see you in court, sir, madam.
	(He is opening the main door when PROSSER suddenly leaps to life and rushes after him.)
PROSSER	In court? You can't go dragging us all into court. I must have professional words with you immediately.
PHOTOGRAPHER	Some other time, sir. Not now.
PROSSER	No, no, no, you don't understand. I'm not like these others. I've got a mother. (Grabbing him by the lapels.) I insist you do not leave this house until I am satisfied as to your bona fide. I warn you I shall even resort to physical violence if necessary.
PHOTOGRAPHER	As you wish, sir. (He does a quick, expert judo move and puts PROSSER flat on his back.) Good morning. (He raises his hat and goes out D.L.)
MELANIE	Oh, do get up, David. This is no time for silly games.
PITT	Yes, do get up, Prosser –
PROSSER	I did warn him. He won't do that again in a hurry.
SIR LINDSAY	You know, it's a pity Prendergast went off with your photo, Grey, otherwise none of this need ever have come out.
MELANIE	Yes, we've all got something on each other: that photograph's the only thing somebody else has got on us.
PITT	(producing a photographic spool from his pocket) Had on us! If you sit on a camera long enough, you'll be amazed what will hatch out of it. Here you are, Grey. Labour's loves lost – and found.
GREY	That's extremely decent of you, Pitt. If there's anything I can do in return –
PITT	There is one thing. When you see Sir Norman

ACT II — UPROAR IN THE HOUSE

	(He puts a finger to his lips.)
GREY	Not a word, naturally. It's all turned out very well, then. We can get back to our beds with a clear conscience.
PITT	Get back to your beds? I'm sorry, not in my – in this house. You seem to forget Sir Lindsay's buying a respectable family home, so don't let us begin anything none of us had any time to start.
	(MISS JOHNSON, YVONNE and LADY COOPER appear in the entrance to the au pair's suite.)
SIR LINDSAY	(coming C. to R. of PITT) Quite right, old chap. We can't have any impropriety. I'm absolutely against that sort of thing. Come along, everyone. Ladies with ladies, men with men.
PROSSER	Where do I go?
PITT	Back in the nursery where you belong. For that matter, we won't have anybody with anybody – we'll all have separate rooms now – except Miss Johnson and Miss Wilby – you'd better make the best of it in the dining room.
	(MISS JOHNSON and YVONNE go, taking PITT's blanket from the tree seat with them.)
	Lady Cooper, you take the master bedroom. Sir Lindsay, you take the second guest room. Mrs. Grey the au pair's suite. Grey – the bathroom for you, and Melanie, you take the first guest room.
MELANIE	All right, darling.
SIR LINDSAY	(as they all go to their respective rooms) But where are you going, old chap?
PITT	(crossing towards the kitchen) There's nothing for it – I shall just have to curl up in the kitchen sink.
SIR LINDSAY	Jolly good. Goodnight – goodnight, Pitt.

	Goodnight, everyone.
ALL	Goodnight. Goodnight.

(PITT switches off all the lights from the switch by the kitchen as all the upstairs and downstairs doors close together. The stage is deserted once more. There is a pause. Then the second guest room and the bathroom doors start to open together and SIR LINDSAY and GREY peer out furtively. They see each other and shoot inside again. There is another short pause, then the bathroom door opens and GREY creeps out. He tiptoes down the stairs and then scuttles into the au pair's suite with evident delight. Now SIR LINDSAY creeps out of the second guest room, does a quick calculation on his fingers to remember where everyone is, and then hastens to the master bedroom. He goes inside with a little chuckle of schoolboy glee. The sliding door to the dining room opens and MISS JOHNSON creeps out. She pauses C., takes a short swig from her brandy flask, straightens her clothes, pats her hair and crosses to the nursery door. She takes off her spectacles as she taps on the door.)

MISS JOHNSON	(calls) Mr. Prosser. Oh, David!

(She goes inside and closes the door.)

(As the nursery door closes, the kitchen door opens and PITT creeps out. He bounds up the stairs and makes for the master bedroom. He remembers just in time and goes straight into the first guest room.)

PITT	It's Romeo!
MELANIE	(off) Hello, Nigel! What kept you?

(As PITT's door closes, there is the sound of a key at the front door. After a moment, the front door opens. LOCKWOOD comes in carrying a picnic hamper and a transistor radio. He crosses to the switch by the kitchen and turns all the lights on.

ACT II	UPROAR IN THE HOUSE	119

LOCKWOOD (going back to the door)   Come in, my dear. Sorry it's taken so long to get here this time. Still, the night is young - and so am I.

(A very attractive, well-dressed WOMAN of about 35 enters.)

WOMAN You don't have to tell me that, Bernard. (She puts her arms round his neck and gives him a light kiss.)   You certainly know how to treat a woman, whatever my husband may think of you.

LOCKWOOD (returning the light kiss)   Not half. Well, it's all work and no play with him, isn't it? You go and freshen yourself up - you know where it is - while I get our little bit of supper ready.

(The WOMAN goes up the stairs on to the landing as LOCKWOOD takes a chicken and a bottle of champagne out of the picnic hamper. She blows him a kiss and he blows one back, holding the champagne bottle in one hand. She goes into the bathroom and closes the door.)

Cor, that's the only good thing I've ever had out of this place - glasses.   (He realises he has no glasses and turns towards the kitchen, picking up the transistor at the same time.) Let's have some music.

(He switches on the transistor. From it come the loud strains of "Oh, you beautiful doll" in cha-cha tempo.)

(He dances out, singing.)   Oh, you beautiful doll, you great big beautiful doll. Let me put my arms around you -

(He disappears singing. As the strains of the music fade away in the kitchen, all the upstairs and downstairs doors open and the occupants creep out, mystified by the latest turn in events.   PITT and MELANIE cross to the centre of the landing.   There is general

	uproar as all concerned realise they have changed rooms again.)
GREY	(pointing to SIR LINDSAY and LADY COOPER) They were at it again – at it again!
SIR LINDSAY	They were in the stable!
PROSSER	(pointing to PITT and MELANIE) They were together – they were together!
PITT	Prosser! Miss Johnson! How could you – in the nursery!
	(LOCKWOOD comes back from the kitchen, singing.)
LOCKWOOD	Oh – oh – oh – OHHHHHH! (He suddenly sees them all and freezes with horror.) Good God, there are dozens of them. What the hell are you doing here, Pitt?
PITT	I might well ask you the same question.
	(There is a violent banging from the bathroom.)
WOMAN	(off) Bernie! Bernie! What's happening, Bernie?
MELANIE	There's somebody locked in the bathroom.
PITT	There can't be – we're all out here – present if not correct.
SIR LINDSAY	Who have you brought to this house, you old rogue?
LOCKWOOD	(noticing him for the first time) Blimey, Sir Lindsay.
	(The WOMAN suddenly manages to yank open the bathroom door and staggers out on to the landing.)
GREY	Good God, it's Isabel!
WOMAN	Mr. Grey! (She notices PITT.) And Mr. Pitt!
PITT	Well, well, well, this is an unexpected pleasure. Good evening, Lady Spens. And how is Sir Norman?
	CURTAIN

UPROAR IN THE HOUSE

Property Plot

Act I, Scene 1

Small tree U.R.C. surrounded by large love seat with a magazine on it - gap between seat and tree big enough for small man to crouch inside

Slim small-bore central heating radiator L. under picture window

Two cone shaped wicker chairs D.R. and U.L.C. covered with dust covers

Low coffee table hewn out of teak U.R.

Built-in television and stereo set U.R.C.

From ceiling D.R., D.L. and U.C. Danish light fittings

Combination telephone table and window-box D.L. (telephone with long lead)

Pipe rack D.L.

Venetian blind on window near main entrance U.L.

Red knob on spiral staircase newel post U.C.

Tall aluminium step ladder marked "Lockwood's Maintenace Dept." standing sideways D.R.

Two open suitcases containing tinned food and artificial flowers D.C.

One valise containing two toothbrushes D.C.

One packing-case containing a photograph of three children (two boys and one girl) D.C. The packing-case is surrounded by wood straw

Toolbag containing a spanner on top of packing-case D.C.

Offstage U.L.
    2 broken bits of glass (ALCOCK)
    1 ballcock complete with armature (ALCOCK)
    Oil-can (MISS JOHNSON)

UPROAR IN THE HOUSE

Offstage D. L.
    Pyjamas in cellophane wrapper (YVONNE)
    Nightdress (YVONNE)
    2 long loaves of French bread (YVONNE)

Offstage D. R.
    Bathbrush (MISS JOHNSON)

Offstage in master bedroom
    Screwdriver (MISS JOHNSON)

Personal

    Large pane of glass (ALCOCK)
    Large abstract painting (MISS JOHNSON)
    Stack of modern square saucepans of different sizes (YVONNE)
    Walking stick (LOCKWOOD)
    Ornate bird cage containing stuffed bird (LOCKWOOD)
    Make-up box (MELANIE)
    Handbag and gloves (LADY COOPER)
    Wallet containing pound note (SIR LINDSAY)

Act I, Scene 2

Same set as Act I, Scene 1, except the dining area is exposed showing the dining room table set for dinner for 4.

Straighten abstract painting

Strike:
    Wood straw on floor
    MELANIE's make-up box
    Magazine on tree-seat

Offstage U. L.
    Soup tureen (MISS JOHNSON)
    Dish of baked potatoes on tray (MISS JOHNSON)
    2 plates of food (MELANIE)
    Steaming saucepan of spaghetti (MELANIE)
    Oven gloves (MELANIE)

Personal
    Watch (PITT)
    Camera (GREY)

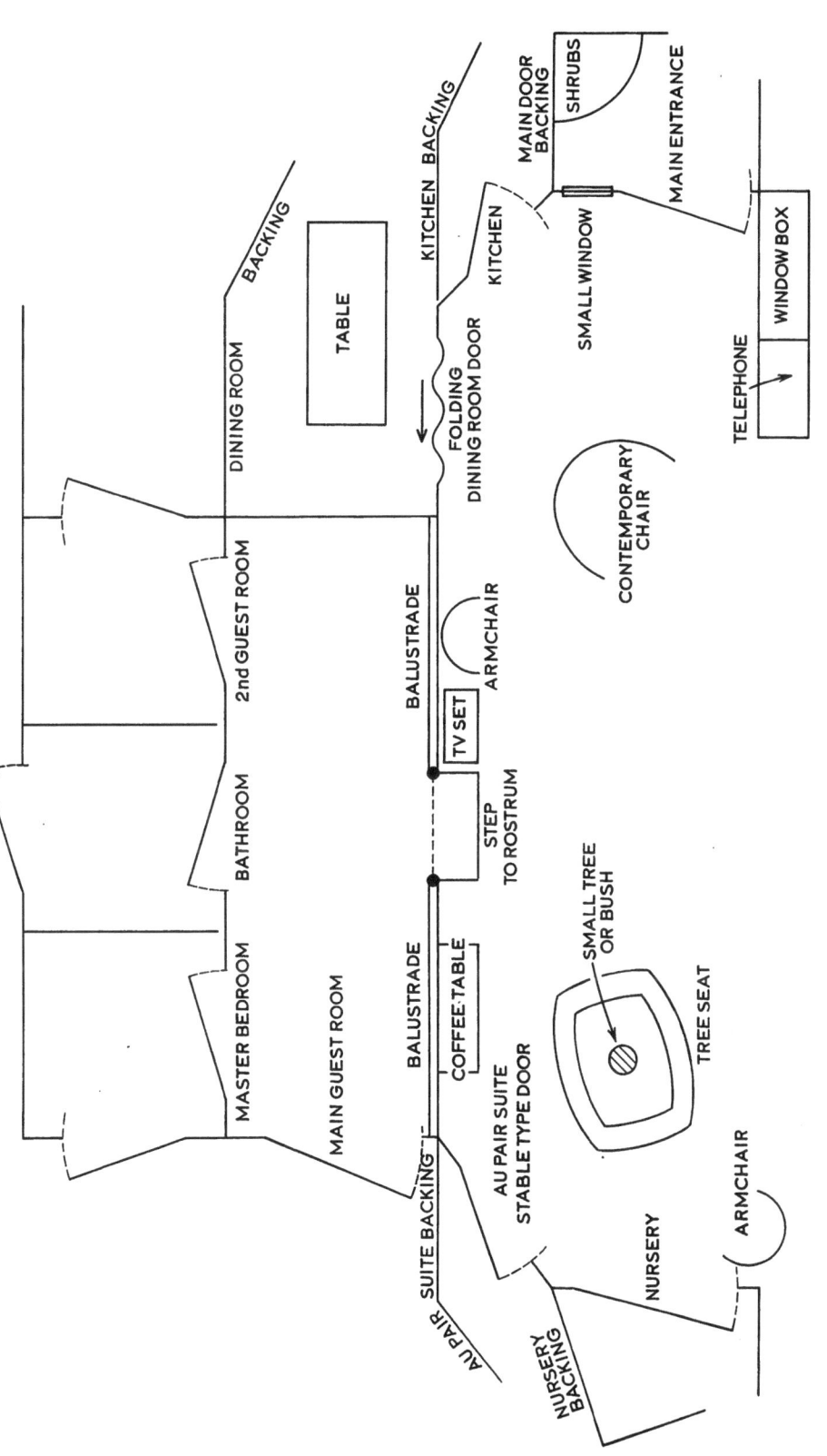

www.ingramcontent.com/pod-product-compliance
Ingram Content Group UK Ltd.
Pitfield, Milton Keynes, MK11 3LW, UK
UKHW021843210426
5322IPUK00022B/435